LIBRARY
2 3 MAY 1997
INFORMATION

RESTAURANT DESIGN—1
SELECTED **AMERICAN RESTAURANTS**

Restaurant Design — 1
— Selected American Restaurants —

Edited by Gen Takeshi Saito

First published in 1992 by
Graphic-sha Publishing Co., Ltd.©
1-9-12, Kudan-kita, Chiyoda-ku, Tokyo 102 Japan
Phone: 81-3-3263-4318
Fax: 81-3-3263-5297

All rights reserved. No part of this publication may be reproduced
or used in any form or by any means — graphic, electronic, or
mechanical, including photocopying, recording, taping, or
information storage and retrieval systems — without written permission
of the publisher.

Printed in Japan by Toppan Printing Co., Ltd.

ISBN 4-7661-0684-9 C-2052

レストラン・デザイン—1
セレクテッド アメリカン・レストラン

Contents

- 11   Ethnic food restaurants
- 63   Italian restaurants
- 95   French restaurants
- 129   Casual & Dinner restaurants-1
- 173   Casual & Dinner restaurants-2
- 217   Fast food & Cafeteria restaurants
- 238   Index

目　次

- 11　エスニック料理レストラン
- 63　イタリア料理レストラン
- 95　フランス料理レストラン
- 129　カジュアル ＆ ディナーレストラン-1
- 173　カジュアル ＆ ディナーレストラン-2
- 217　ファストフード ＆ カフェテリアレストラン
- 238　インデックス

FOREWORD

More than 20 years have already passed since I began to photograph American restaurants. It was the autumn of 1968 that I first went to America. In those days, I remember, a passport was effective for only one round of foreign travel and an application had to be filed to bring out foreign currency, and everything I saw, heard and ate was a series of surprises to me. The fast food and family restaurant chains were just developing as major waves, and "McDonald," "Kentucky Fried Chicken," "Shakey's," "Denny's," "Big Boy," "Sambo's" which later disappeared, and other chains looked wonderful to us. It was in the latter half of the 1960s that many people from Japan went over to America to observe those wonderful chains, learned much, and were stimulated. Starting with the introduction of systems, methods for rationalization and manuals, they have mastered the basics from which today's prosperous restaurant business in Japan has developed.

In July 1971 when the first "McDonald" in Japan opened in "Mitsukoshi," Ginza, Tokyo, it aroused a sensation. In those days, the native family restaurant chain "Skylark" was also consolidating its foundation. In the early years of the 1970s, the mainstream of shop making in America and Japan had been based on the pursuit of uniform design and rationalized systems. Since then, brand-new concepts, trends and temporary fashions have affected American dining-out styles and eating habits, making themselves felt in the 1980s as major factors in change. These changes looked as if a food revolution was taking place in America, and a variety of trendy foods appeared — Californian, Mexican, Cajun, Southwestern, Thai, Chinese and other Asian foods, as well as Caribbean, Mediterranean and other ethnic cuisine. Behind them one finds sudden increases in immigrants into America in the 1980s, and the eating culture brought in by newcomers from Mexico and Asia, among other places, has created an ethnic food boom, and these foods have successfully assimilated on the American soil and have been accepted as "American foods" in a broad sense. Cooks have come from different parts of the world, and are creating new types of food as they encounter new materials in different parts of America and fuse their native foods with others. In the 1990s the American food industry is continuing to change greatly, and generating innovative shop presentations and design concepts.

Over the past ten years I have collected data on several hundred restaurants, and from that collection I have selected 112 of them which have characteristic designs and topical concepts, and classified them by type of business or operation into ●ethnic food restaurants ●Italian restaurants ●French restaurants ●casual & dinner restaurants ●fast food & cafeteria restaurants, and have mainly introduced their interiors. I also included restaurants which have since been closed within the last ten years, if their designs remain interesting and meaningful even today. The common features of these restaurants are as follows:

● **Ethnic food restaurants**

America has been called a melting pot of races, and consequently new-types of foreign foods and ethnic culture have been introduced and accepted. In the 1980s these movements made themselves felt as an ethnic boom which has continued to date. In this category I have included the Caribbean, Mexican, Chinese, Polynesian, Japanese and other restaurants whose dishes and concepts are worthy of attention.

● **Italian restaurants**

In New York there are many Italian immigrants, and therefore many Italian restaurants which usually feature traditional shop designs and foods local to different parts of Italy, but there also are recently designed restaurants such as "Remi" and "Trattoria Dell'Arte."

● **French restaurants**

Although many French restaurants are of the high-class variety whose owners, chefs and employees are also French, American chefs have been cooking for the last few years and are beginning to cook confidently in the American French restaurant industry.

● **Casual & dinner restaurants**

All restaurants featured in this category exhibit concepts which were freely hit upon — i.e. characteristic of Americans — and have a rich variety of foods on the menu. Thus, they come in the style most acceptable to Americans. Naturally, those introduced in this category are the largest number in the book.

● **Fast food & cafeteria restaurants**

Although many restaurant designs were standardized in the 1970s, designers have delved into original concepts in the 1980s, presenting a diverse variety of elements. "Food courts" in shopping centers, among others concepts, are the most notable. Since a variety of ethnic foods have appeared, it has become necessary to gather various restaurants from different countries in one place so that people can select and enjoy the foods they prefer. This type of 'cuisine center' is increasingly drawing attention.

April 1992

Gen Takeshi Saito

はじめに

アメリカのレストラン業界を見続けて早や20年以上が経過した。初めてアメリカに出かけたのが1968年の秋であったが　当時の海外渡航は　1回限りのパスポートしか発行されず　外貨の持ち出しも申請しなければならなかったことを思い出す。そして見るもの　聞くもの　食べるものなどの全てが驚きの連続であった。ちょうど　ファストフードやファミリーレストランのチェーンが大きなウェーブを起こして発展を続けている時でもあり　"マクドナルド"や"ケンタッキー フライドチキン""シェイキーズ""デニーズ""ビッグ ボーイ"そして後に消滅してしまった"サンボス"などが　我々の目にすばらしく映ったものである。日本からは多くの人たちがこれらの業界のすばらしさを見に出かけ　多くの事柄を学び　刺激されてきたのも60年代半ばからであった。システムや合理化　マニュアルといったものの導入から始まり　今日の隆盛する飲食業界を生み出す基礎造りを学んだといえる。

1971年7月に"マクドナルド"の日本進出1号店が東京　銀座の"三越"にオープンした時の反響は大変大きなものであったが　日本生まれのファミリー レストラン"すかいらーく"もその基礎を固めていた時代である。1970年代初期における店舗と造りは　デザインの画一化と　システムの合理化の追求が日米でも主流であった。以来　数多くの斬新なコンセプトやトレンド　そして一時的な流行などがアメリカの外食様式と食習慣に影響を与え　1980年代に大きな変化となって表れた。それはアメリカのフード革命とでもいえるほどで　トレンディな料理が登場し　カリフォルニア　メキシカン　ケイジャン　サウスウエスト　タイ　中国その他アジア料理　カリブ　地中海料理など多種多様の料理が出現した。その背景には1980年代になり　アメリカへの移住が急増したことがある。特にメキシコやアジアからの新しい住民によって運び込まれた食文化が　エスニック フードの流行をもたらしたといえる。そして　これらの料理がアメリカの土壌にうまく同化し　広い意味での"アメリカ料理"として認められてきた。料理人も世界の各地からアメリカに集まり　アメリカ各地の新しい食材との出会いや　各国の料理との融合による新しい料理も生まれてきている。1990年代にかけてのアメリカのフード業界の10年間は　大きく変化しなお変化し続けている期間であり　店舗の演出やデザインにも革新的なコンセプトを生み出している。

本書では　過去10年間に取材した数百にも及ぶレストランの中から　特徴のあるデザインや話題のコンセプトを持つ112店をセレクトし　業種　業態別に●エスニック料理レストラン　●イタリア料理レストラン　●フランス料理レストラン　●カジュアル＆ディナーレストラン　●ファストフード＆カフェテリアレストランに分類し　インテリアを中心に紹介するものとした。また　10年の間にすでに閉店されてしまったレストランでも　面白さが見られ　現在にも通じるデザインの店は敢えてここに収録した。掲載されたレストランの内容は下記の通りである。

●エスニック料理レストラン
人種のるつぼといわれるアメリカに新しい外国の料理や異文化が導入され　受け入れられている。1980年代にはエスニックブームとなって表れ　現在も継続している。カリブ　メキシカン　チャイニーズ　タパス　ジャパニーズなど　それぞれの料理とコンセプトが注目されるレストランを集めた。

●イタリア料理レストラン
ニューヨークは　特にイタリア系住民が多いところでありイタリア料理レストランも多い。イタリア各地の伝統的な料理や　店造りがみられるが"REMI"や"TRATTORIA DELL'ARTE"など全く新しいデザインの店もある。

●フランス料理レストラン
フランス料理レストランは高級店が多く　シェフ　オーナー　従業員などフランス人が多いなかで　ここ数年間でアメリカ生まれのシェフたちがそだち　アメリカの料理界にも一段とその自信が見えはじめた。

●カジュアル＆ディナーレストラン
ここに集めたどのレストランも　アメリカらしい自由な発想のコンセプトで　メニューも多種多彩。そしてアメリカ人に最も親しまれるスタイルである。したがって本書の中での収録数が最も多い。

●ファストフード＆カフェテリアレストラン
1970年代の画一化されたデザインも　1980年代になり独創性が追求され　コンセプトの多様化が続く。中でも注目されるのが　ショッピングセンター内のフードコートである。エスニック料理の登場で　各国の様々な料理店を1カ所に集め　各々が好む料理を選んで楽しめる　そんな場所の提供がクローズアップされている。

1992年4月　斎藤　武

エスニック料理レストラン

バヤモ〈ニューヨーク〉 12
カフェ イグアナ〈ニューヨーク〉 14
レベッカ〈カリフォルニア・ヴェニス〉 16
カサ ガヤード〈フロリダ・オーランド〉 18
チャイナ グリル〈ニューヨーク〉 20
エル テディーズ〈ニューヨーク〉 22
エル インターナショナル〈ニューヨーク〉 24
チャ チャ チャ〈ロサンゼルス〉 26
エル トリート〈カリフォルニア・ビバリーヒルズ〉 28
サルード〈カリフォルニア・ハンティントンビーチ〉 30
トミー タン〈ニューヨーク〉 32
エル モカンボ〈ロサンゼルス〉 34
ドン ホセ〈カリフォルニア・トーランス〉 36
ザ レッドオニオン〈カリフォルニア・ハンティントンビーチ〉 38
アカプルコ イ ロス アルコス〈カリフォルニア・ラークスパー〉 40
ザ レッドオニオン〈カリフォルニア・マリナ デル レイ〉 42
カフェ バ・バ・リーバ〈シカゴ〉 44
京樽〈カリフォルニア・ダウニー〉 46
吉祥庵〈ロサンゼルス〉 48
カンサイ寿司割烹〈カリフォルニア・サンタモニカ〉 50
ベニハナ カフェ〈ニューヨーク〉 52
チャイナ クラブ〈ロサンゼルス〉 54
赤坂飯店〈ロサンゼルス〉 56
香蘭厨〈ロサンゼルス〉 58
チョップスティック〈ロサンゼルス〉 60

Ethnic food restaurants

BAYAMO ⟨New York⟩ 12
CAFE IGUANA ⟨New York⟩ 14
REBECCA'S ⟨Venice, CA.⟩ 16
CASA GALLARDO ⟨Orlando, Florida⟩ 18
CHINA GRILL ⟨New York⟩ 20
EL TEDDY'S ⟨New York⟩ 22
EL INTERNACIONAL ⟨New York⟩ 24
CHA CHA CHA ⟨Los Angeles⟩ 26
EL TORITO ⟨Beverly Hills, CA.⟩ 28
SALUD ⟨Huntington Beach, CA.⟩ 30
TOMMY TANG'S ⟨New York⟩ 32
EL MOCAMBO ⟨Los Angeles⟩ 34
DON JOSE ⟨Torrance, CA.⟩ 36
THE RED ONION ⟨Huntington Beach, CA.⟩ 38
ACAPULCO Y LOS ARCOS ⟨Larkspur, CA.⟩ 40
THE RED ONION ⟨Marina Del Rey, CA.⟩ 42
CAFE BA·BA·REEBA! ⟨Chicago⟩ 44
KYOTARU ⟨Downey, CA.⟩ 46
KISHO-AN ⟨Los Angeles⟩ 48
KANSAI SUSHI KAPPO ⟨Santa Monica, CA.⟩ 50
BENIHANA CAFE ⟨New York⟩ 52
CHINA CLUB ⟨Los Angeles⟩ 54
AKASAKA HANTEN ⟨Los Angeles⟩ 56
FRAGRANT VEGETABLE RESTAURANT ⟨Los Angeles⟩ 58
CHOPSTIX ⟨Los Angeles⟩ 60

BAYAMO ⟨New York⟩

In New York there are young professionals called "yuppies" and they like to visit East Village and Lower Broadway in the south of Manhattan. "Bayamo" is an ethnic food restaurant situated in Lower Broadway. "Bayamo" is the name of a town in Cuba, and the cuisine served here is a unique mixture of Latin and Chinese foods accented with a spicy taste. In the restaurant, which uses a remodeled warehouse, finely designed columns and large wall art by the entrance accentuate the high space. The corrugated bar counter is eye-catching.

● BAYAMO (New York)
Address/707 Broadway North of 4th Street New York, N.Y.
Phone/212-475-5151
Opened/April, 1985;   Number of seats/300;
Number of employees/65

ニューヨークで若い専門職"ヤッピー"とよばれる人たちが好んで出かける地域は　マンハッタン島の南部　イースト ビレッジやローアー ブロードウェイなどだが　「バヤモ」は そんな場所に位置するエスニック料理レストラン。店名はキューバの町の名に由来している。料理はラテン料理と中国料理が融合され　それにスパイシィな味が加わった独特のもの。倉庫を改装した店内はデザインされた円柱と　入口近くの大きなウォール アートが高い空間を強調している。波をうったバーカウンターの演出もおもしろい。

●バヤモ〈ニューヨーク〉
Address/707 Broadway North of 4th Street New York, N.Y.　Phone/212-475-5151　開店/1985年4月　客席数/300席　従業員数/65人

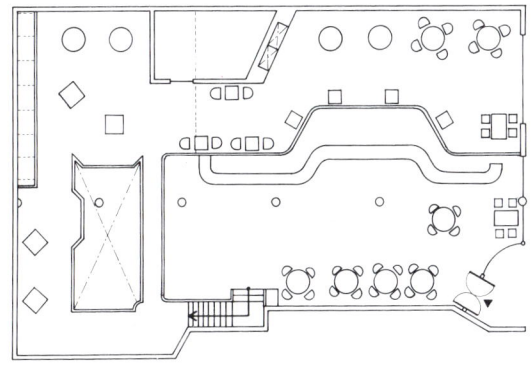

(Photo captions)
1 / The interior features decorated columns and avant-garde wall art.
2 / The 2nd floor dining area introducing the deformative flows, and the 1st floor corrugated bar counter.
3 / The wall art painted fully in the high space.

1/店内は装飾された円柱と前衛的なウォールアートが印象的
2/変形の流れを導入した2階ダイニングエリアと波形の1階カウンター
3/高い空間いっぱいに描かれたウォールアート

CAFE IGUANA 〈New York〉

Situated in the South of Midtown, Manhattan, "Cafe Iguana" derived the name from "The Night of Iguana," a movie that has most charmed the owner Joyce Steins, and the interior reproduces its scenes. The wide dining area has a tropical atmosphere, and the floor is composed like a stage accented with multi-colored lighting and an eye-catching brass-made iguana which is as long as 10 feet.. The restaurant mainly serves casual Tex-Mex and grill dishes.
● CAFE IGUANA (New York)
Address/235 Park Avenue (South at 19th Street) New York, N.Y. 10003
Phone/212-529-4770
Opened/January 1988; Number of seats/300 (dining area only)

マンハッタンのミッドタウンの南に位置する「カフェ イグアナ」の店名は オーナーのJoyce Steinsさんが最も魅了された映画"イグアナの夜"に由来し インテリアにもそのシーンが再現されている。広いダイニングエリアはトロピカルな雰囲気で ステージ状にフロア構成され 色とりどりの照明と10フィートもある真鍮製のイグアナが目をひく。料理はカジュアルなTex Mexとグリルがメイン。
●カフェ イグアナ〈ニューヨーク〉
Address/235 Park Avenue South at 19th Street New York, N.Y.10003 Phone/212-529-4770
開店/1988年1月 客席数/300席（ダイニングエリアのみ）

(Photo captions)
1 / The scenes of the movie "The Night of Iguana" are reproduced on the spacious floor, 900 square feet (about 836.1 m²). Climbing the central staircase, one reaches the tropical bar, restaurant, cancun room, etc.
2 / The 1st floor bar corner. The crystal iguana eyes (lighting) stand out very impressively.

1/900平方フィート（約836.1㎡）の広い空間に 映画"イグアナの夜(Night of Iguana)"のシーンを再現 中央部の階段を上がると2階のトロピカルバー レストラン カンクンルームなどに続く
2/1階バーコーナー クリスタル製のイグアナの目（照明）が一段とひきたつ

REBECCA'S 〈Venice, CA.〉

With the presentation of strange aquatic images, "Rebecca's" is a Mexican restaurant designed by Frank Gehry, and its owner-chef Bruce Marder offers new-style Mexican cuisine. Two huge crocodiles about 19 feet (5.7 m) and a giant octopus are suspended from the ceiling, while light is cast so that the wall surface stands out, thereby expressing aquatic fantasy. Situated in Venice in the south of Santa Monica, the restaurant is frequented by artists, yuppies, etc.
● REBECCA'S (Venice, CA.)
Address/2025 Pacific Avenue Venice, CA. 90028
Phone/213-306-6266;
Opened/May 1986;   Number of seats/160
Number of employees/70

アクアティック(水中)の風変わりなイメージを演出した「レベッカ」は Frank Gehryがデザインしたメキシカンレストラン。オーナーシェフのBruce Marder氏が 新しいスタイルのメキシコ料理を提供している。19フィート(約5.7m)もあるワニやジャイアント オクトパス(蛸)をダイニングエリアの天井に泳がせたり 照明で壁面を浮き出させたりして 水中のファンタジィを表現している。サンタモニカの南のヴェニス(Venice)地区に位置し アーティストやヤッピーたちを客層としている。
●レベッカ〈カリフォルニア・ヴェニス〉
Address/2025 Pacific Avenue Venice, CA.90028
Phone/213-306-6266 開店/1986年5月 客席数/160席 従業員数/70人

(Photo captions)
1・2/ The guest seating area with a giant octopus and huge crocodiles (5.7 m long), gives a strange impression.
3 / The entrance features onyx and a uniquely designed door.

1・2/天井に巨大な蛸(ジャイアント オクトパス)や 5.7mもあるワニを配した客席の雰囲気は異様な感じを与える
3/オニックス材とユニークなデザインのドアがあるエントランス

CASA GALLARDO ⟨Orlando, Florida⟩

A Mexican restaurant chain headquartered in St. Louis, "Casa Gallardo" means the house of Mr. Gallardo, owner. The interior uses the terrace of a Mexican building as its theme, and the pieces of furniture, fresco design and colors may be said to be the very essence of Mexico. The main customers are adult couples aged 18〜45.
- CASA GALLARDO (Orlando, Florida)
Address/8250 International Drive Orland, Florida 32809
Opened/January 1983; Number of seats/400 (dining 300, bar 100); Number of employees/140

(Photo captions)
1 / The dining area's interior reminds one of a Mexican residence.
2 / The dining area imaging a patio.
3 / The colorfully presented bar corner.

1/メキシコの邸宅を思わせるダイニングのインテリア
2/パティオをイメージしたダイニング エリア
3/カラフルな演出のバーコーナー

セントルイスに本拠を置きチェーン展開しているメキシカンレストラン。店名はオーナーのガヤード(Gallardo)氏の家という意味の「カサ ガヤード」。店名はメキシコの建物のテラスをテーマにしており 家具や調度品 壁画のデザイン 色彩などメキシコそのものと言った感じ。客層は18〜45才までのアダルト カップルが中心。
- カサ ガヤード⟨フロリダ・オーランド⟩
Address/8250 International Drive Orlando, Florida 32809　開店/1983年1月　客席数/400席 (ダイニング300席　バー100席)　従業員数/140人

②

③

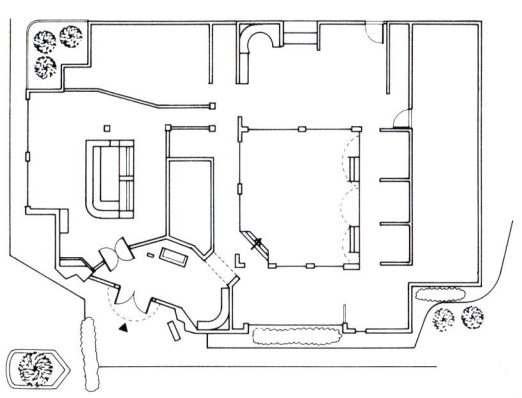

CHINA GRILL 〈New York〉

An "international food" restaurant opened by Japanese chef Mako Tanaka, "China Grill" serves cuisine by blending Californian foods with Japanese, Chinese, Indonesian, Vietnamese and French foods. The interior decor is impressive with an oval lampshade under the high ceiling which reminds us of Japanese 'shoji' (sliding paper screen), agreeing well with the moderate wall colors. The floor space is composed of a guest seating area in several partitions, an open kitchen in the center, slender bar counters on both sides, etc.

● CHINA GRILL (New York)
Address/60 West 53rd Street, between 5th & 6th Avenue, New York, U.Y. 10019
Phone/212-333-7788
Opened/September 1987;　　Number of seats/225 (dining 185, bar 40);　Number of employees/125

日本人シェフ　田中誠人(Mako Tanaka)氏の"インターナショナル フード"レストラン。料理は日本　中国　インドネシア　ヴェトナム　フランス料理に　カリフォルニア料理をブレンドしたもの。店内は高い天井空間に障子を思わせる楕円形のランプシェードが印象的で　おさえ気味の壁面カラーにマッチしている。幾つかに分けられた客席と中央部のオープンキッチン　その両側の細長いバーカウンターなどで構成されている。

●チャイナ グリル〈ニューヨーク〉
Address/60 West 53rd Street, between 5th & 6th Avenue, New York, N.Y. 10019　Phone/212-333-7788　開店/1987年9月　客席数/225席（ダイニング185席　バー40席）　従業員数/125人

(Photo captions)
1 / Using different floor levels and ceiling height effectively, the dining area is accented with a lampshade which images Japanese 'shoji.'
2 / The dining area by the entrance viewed from the bar counter.
3 / The bar counter and open kitchen; on the straight line drawn across the floor leading into the inner dining area, sentences from Marco Polo's "Book of Marco Polo" (Record of Experiences in the East) are written.

1/フロアに段差をつけ　天井の高さをうまく利用したダイニングエリア　ランプシェードは障子をイメージしている
2/バーカウンターからエントランス脇のダイニングをみる
3/バーカウンターとオープンキッチン　フロアに引かれたラインにはマルコ ポーロの〈東方見聞録〉が書かれ奥のダイニングへと続いている

EL TEDDY'S ⟨New York⟩

A Mexican restaurant opened in Tribeca by Mr. Andrew Young and Cristopher Chesnutt, "El Teddy's" mainly serves traditional Mexican foods, plus a menu which changes from day to day, vegetarian foods, etc. Since 1925 when the building was used by Teddy who opened a cafeteria, it has been used for various types of restaurant, such as steak and tapas. The facade is unique with a huge crown of the Statue of Liberty placed on the roof, which has been taken over from the tapas restaurant "El Internacional" (see page 24) which opened in the mid-1980s and was hotly talked about in those days. The interior retains the tiled frescos and mosaic walls in the cafeteria days which, coupled with modern artistic pieces, produce a unique atmosphere.

● EL TEDDY'S (New York)
Address/219 West Broadway New York, N.Y. 10013
Phone/212-941-7070
Opened/January 1988;   Number of seats/100;   Number of employees/30

アンドリュー ヤング(Andrew Young)氏とクリストファー チェスナット(Cristpher Chesnutt)氏が トライベッカ(Tribeca)にオープンしたメキシカンレストラン。料理は伝統的なメキシコ料理を中心に 日変わりやベジタリアン向けのメニューなど。この建物はテディーという人が 1925年にカフェテリアを開店して以来 ステーキハウス タパス料理など種々のレストランに経営が変わった歴史あるもの。ファサードは自由の女神の巨大なクラウンを屋根の上に乗せたユニークなものでこれは1980年代半ばにオープンし話題になったタパス料理レストラン「エル インターナショナル(El Internacional)」(本書24ページ収録)のそれを引き継いだもの。店内はカフェテリア当時のタイルの壁画やモザイクの壁が残されており それらとモダンアート感覚の作品が新しい雰囲気を醸し出している。

●エル テディーズ〈ニューヨーク〉
Address/219 West Broadway New York, N.Y. 10013 Phone/212-941-7070 開店/1988年1月 客席数/100席 従業員数/30人

(Photo captions)
1 / The facade retaining some vestige of "El Internacional" whose tapas cuisine was hotly talked about in the 1980s; features a symbol designed by imaging the crown of the Statue of Liberty.
2・3 / The dining room.
4 / The staircase handrails made by using scrap iron, register, etc., and two barbecue skewers are hanged on the wall.
5・6・7 / Pieces of modern art are displayed.

1/1980年代 タパス料理で話題の「El Internacional」の面影を残すファサード 自由の女神のクラウンをイメージしたデザイン
2・3/ダイニングルーム
4/廃材の鉄やレジスターを使用した階段の手摺り 壁面にはバーベキューの串が掛けられている
5～7/店内には現代アートの作品が展示されている

④

⑤

⑥

⑦

EL INTERNACIONAL ⟨New York⟩

"El Internacional" was a tapas restaurant which serves a variety of foods, each in small volume. "Tapas" is a group of foods local to Cataluña district centering around Barcelona, Spain, and mainly features fish and eggs cooked by steaming, broiling or frying, and seasoned with olive oil, vinegar, etc. Although Tapas is originally intended to be served between meals, "El Internacional" served it as the main dish which was favorably accepted by "hot" New Yorkers such as designers, artists, young professionals, etc. The facade looks like that of Gaudi's work of art, designed by imaging the Statue of Liberty. With a highly fashionable sense, the interior was designed by Antoni Miralda. The restaurant was closed and taken over by the Mexican restaurant "El Teddy's" (see page 22).

● EL INTERNACIONAL (New York)
Closed now; Number of seats/211 (1st floor 125, 2nd floor 54, bar 32); Number of employees/50

(Photo captions)
1 / The facade whose design reminds us of Gaudi.
2 / The bar lounge; the bar counter reflected in the wall mirror.
3 / The bar counter; the suspended eating materials and small plates attached to lighting are interesting.
4 / The entrance hall; the floor and lampshade designed with the flags of all nations.

1/ガウディを思わせるデザインのファサード
2/バーラウンジ 壁面のミラーにバーカウンターが映り込んでいる
3/バーカウンター ぶら下げられた食材や照明に取りつけられた小皿がおもしろい
4/エントランスホール 床やランプシェードには万国旗がデザインされている

少量の料理をいろいろ食べさせるタパス(tapas)料理レストラン。タパスはスペインのバルセロナを中心にしたカタルナ(Cataluña)地方の料理で 魚介類や卵料理が多く 調理方法は蒸す 焼く 揚げるなど様々で オリーブ油や酢などの調味料を使う。もともとは間食用のものだが「エル インターナショナル」ではメインディッシュとして提供し デザイナーやアーティスト 専門職などホットなニューヨーカーたちの人気を得た。このレストランはガウディ(Gaudi)のような外観で 自由の女神をイメージしたもの。ハイファッション感覚で インテリアはアントニィ ミラルダ(Antoni Miralda)氏が手掛けたが 現在は閉店し メキシカンレストランの「エル テディーズ(El Teddy's)」(本書22ページ収録)になっている。

●エル インターナショナル〈ニューヨーク〉
現在閉店中 客席数/211席(1F125席 2F54席 バー32席) 従業員数/50人

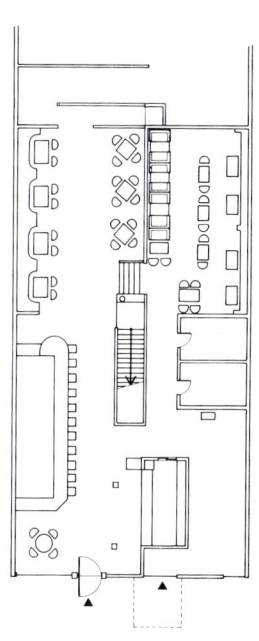

CHA CHA CHA ⟨Los Angeles⟩

"Cha Cha Cha" is a Caribbean restaurant — very rare even in Los Angeles where many ethnic restaurants are operating. Situated at a corner near the eastern end of Melrose Avenue, the facade in bright sky blue stands out. The colors of not merely the wall and ceiling but also table cloth and even pictures on the wall are coordinated based mainly on the blue tint, and accented with fresh flowers, thus creating the typical Caribbean fragrance.

● CHA CHA CHA (Los Angeles)
Address/656 N. Virgil Avenue, Los Angeles, CA. 90004
Phone/213-664-7723
Opened/June 1986;   Number of seats/74 (table 49, patio 25);   Number of employees/23

エスニックレストランが多いロサンゼルスでも珍しいカリブ料理レストラン。ユニークなブティックが並ぶメルロース通り(Melrose Avenue)の 東のはずれに近い一角に位置する。明るい青色の空のファサードが一段と目をひく。店内は壁や天井 テーブルクロス 壁面の絵の色までブルーをポイントにコーディネイトされ 生花でアクセントをつけ カリブの香りを感じさせる。

●チャ チャ チャ ⟨ロサンゼルス⟩
Address/656 N.Virgil Avenue Los Angeles, CA. 90004 Phone/213-664-7723 開店/1986年6月 客席数/74席(テーブル49席 パティオ25席) 従業員数/23人

①

②

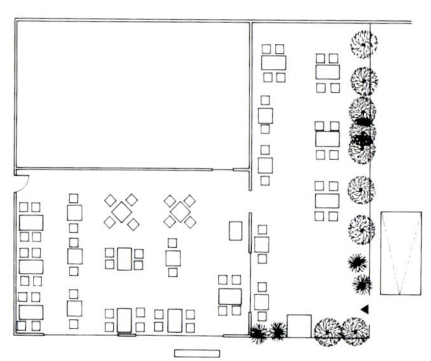

(Photo captions)
1 / The reception with an antique clock and uniquely designed stool.
2 / The bright Caribbean blue facade.
3 / The open dining area in which one can feel the Caribbean sun and wind, accented with the Caribbean blue.

1/レセプション アンティークな時計やユニークなデザインのスツールが置かれている
2/明るいカリブブルーのファサード
3/カリブの太陽と風を感じさせる開放的なダイニング カリブブルーがポイント

EL TORITO 〈Beverly Hills, CA.〉

Affiliated with the Restaurant Enterprise Group, "El Torito" is the largest Mexican restaurant chain in America. "El Torito Beverly Hills" stresses a Southwestern atmosphere with blue as the basic tone. The ceiling features a painting expressing dynamic images of the expansive and vivid blue sky drawn by Mr. Dale Ter Bush who undertook the design. The menu contains unique foods such as Southwestern, Tex-Mex and Californian.

● EL TORITO (Beverly Hills, CA.)
Address/9595 Wilshire Boulevard Beverly Hills, CA. 90210
Phone/213-550-1599
Opened/July 1989;   Number of seats/288 (dining 240, bar corner 48)

「エル トリート」は レストランエンタープライズグループ社傘下で チェーン展開をすすめるアメリカ最大のメキシカンレストランである。このビバリーヒルズ店はブルーを基調にサウスウエスタンの雰囲気を強調 メインダイニングの天井には設計を担当したDale Terbush氏が描いた鮮やかな青空の絵が広がり ダイナミックなイメージを表現している。メニューはサウスウエスタン テックスメックス（Tax-Mex） カリフォルニアなどの特徴ある料理を提供している。

●エル トリート〈カリフォルニア・ビバリーヒルズ〉
Address/9595 Wilshire Boulevard Beverly Hills, CA．Phone/213-550-1599　開店/1989年7月　客席数/288席（ダイニング240席　バーコーナー48席）

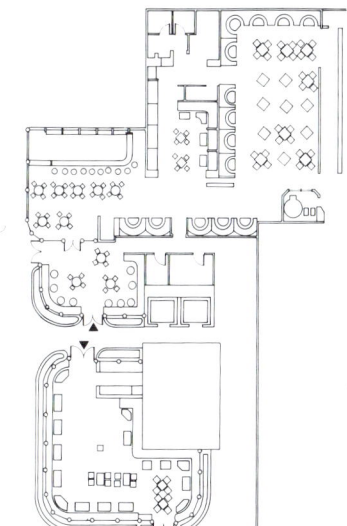

(Photo captions)
1 / The main dining room; on the ceiling, the clear blue sky is painted expressing dynamic images.
2 / The exotic and dignified bar corner.
3 / The main entrance; the bar corner is visible behind the cactus.

1/メインダイニング 天井には鮮やかな青空が描かれダイナミックなイメージが表現されている
2/エキゾチックで格調のあるバーコーナー
3/メインエントランス カクタスの向こうにバーコーナーが見える

SALUD 〈Huntington Beach, CA.〉

②

③

The shop name "Salud" is a Spanish word of greeting meaning "I pray for your health" and bases its concept on Mexican Indian culture. Managed by Mr. Larry Cano. The design was undertaken by Mr. Dale Ter Bush who successfully redecorated the former Italian restaurant into a colorful theatrical restaurant. With emphasis on an open, familiar atmosphere, the open kitchen and cooking equipment are placed near the shop front for show-like presentation so that guests can enjoy cooking scenes.
● SALUD (Huntington Beach, CA.)
Address/11707 Beach Boulevard Huntington Beach, CA. 92647
Phone/714-842-1194
Opened/June 1989; Number of seats/326 (restaurant 229, patio 54, bar 43); Number of employees/70

店名の「サルード」は"あなたの健康を祈る"という意味のスペイン語の挨拶に由来する。メキシカン インディアンをコンセプトにしたレストラン。経営はLarry Cano氏。デザインはDale Terbush氏で 元イタリアンレストランだったこの店舗をカラフルな劇場風に改装した。開放感や親近感を重視し オープンキッチンや器具などを店頭近くに置き 調理を客に見せて楽しませるショー風な演出をしている。
●サルード〈カリフォルニア・ハンティントンビーチ〉
Address/11707 Beach Boulevard Huntington Beach, CA.924647 Phone/714-842-1194 開店/1989年6月 客席数/326席(レストラン229席 パティオ54席 バー43席) 従業員/70人

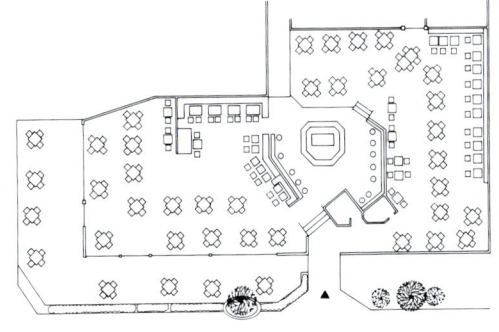

(Photo captions)
1 / The deep, bright dining room.
2 / The bar corner: accented with overhead cactuses.
3 / The reception near the entrance and the booth with an oven.
4 / The free-standing facade.

1/奥行きのある明るいダイニングルーム
2/バーコーナー 頭上に植えられたカクタスがおもしろい
3/エントランス近くのレセプションとオーブンが置かれたブース
4/フリースタンディングのファサード

TOMMY TANG'S ⟨New York⟩

"Tommy Tang's" is a Thai restaurant popular for the unique seasoning and artistic dishing up by the owner-chef Tommy Tang who was born in Bangkok. In sharp contrast to location in modern highrise buildings such as the World Trade Center, it is situated in a warehouse quarter of Tribeca area. In the restaurant under the high ceiling, the walls are used to display pieces of art periodically brought in by artists so that the interior has an atmosphere like that of an art gallery. The dining area is frequented by those involved in fashion or music business and also by young professionals who can have an unobstructed view.

● TOMMY TANG'S (New York)
Address/323 Greenwich Street New York, N.Y. 10013
Phone/212-334-9190
Opened/October 1986;   Number of seats/100 (dining 90, bar 10)

バンコック生まれのオーナーシェフ　トミータンの斬新な味付けと芸術的盛り付けで人気のタイ料理レストラン。ワールドトレードセンターなどの近代的な高層ビルとは　対照的なトライベッカ(Tribeca)地区の倉庫街の一画にある。高い天井空間の店内は　壁面にアーティストたちによって定期的に持ち込まれる作品が飾られアートギャラリーのような雰囲気で　見通し良く構成されたダイニングエリアには　ファッションやミュージック関係　若いプロフェッショナルたちが集まる。

●トミータン〈ニューヨーク〉
Address/323 Greenwich Street New York, N.Y. 10013　Phone/212-334-9190　開店/1986年10月　客席数/100席（ダイニング90席　バー10席）

(Photo captions)
1 / The facade situated in a warehouse quarter of Tribeca where a quiet atmosphere remains in contrast to the World Trade Center which stands away from the quarter.
2 / The inner corner under a top light is placed at a level a little higher than the rest of the floor, and allows guests to enjoy an unobstructed view.
3 / The dining area having an atmosphere of art gallery.

1/トライベッカ(Tribeca)の倉庫街にあるファサード　後方のワールドトレードセンターとは対象的にまだ静寂感が残っている地域
2/トップライトを取り入れた奥のコーナーは一段高く見通しの良い構成にしている
3/アートギャラリーの雰囲気を持つダイニングエリア

EL MOCAMBO 〈Los Angeles〉

A Cuban restaurant opened by the owner Perry Santos by inviting Mr. Toribio Prado, who is active at "Cha Cha Cha" (see page 26), etc., as consultant chef. It introduces tropical trees into the interior, and fans are suspended from the ceiling which features a skylight. On the wall illustrations are drawn in bright colors and natural light comes in the inner terrace dining area, thus presenting a bright atmosphere of the Caribbean Sea. "EL MOCAMBO" is crowded with guests from Beverly Hills, West Hollywood, etc.
● EL MOCAMBO (Los Angeles)
Address/8338 W. Third Street Los Angeles, CA. 90048
Phone/213-651-2113
Opened/February 1989;   Number of seats/ 120～150 (dining 90～120, bar 30)

オーナーのPerry Santos氏が「チャ チャ チャ(Cha Cha Cha)」(本書26ページ収録)などで活躍するToribio Prado氏をコンサルタント シェフに迎え オープンしたキューバ料理レストラン。トロピカル調の樹木をインテリアに取り入れ 天窓のある天井からは扇風機が下がる。壁面に明るい色で描かれたイラストがあり 自然光のさしこむ店内奥のテラスダイニングなどカリブ海の持つ明るい雰囲気が演出されておりビバリーヒルズやハリウッドの客で賑わっている。
●エル モカンボ〈ロサンゼルス〉
Address/8338 W.Third Street Los Angeles, CA.90048 Phone/213-651-2113 開店/1989年2月 客席数/120～150席(ダイニング90～120席 バー30席)

(Photo captions)
1 / The round table in the center of the main dining area; the wall mirror looks like a window.
2 / The bar corner in a tropical mood.
3 / The bar; the large mirror on the wall also features a tropical design.
4 / The terrace dining area under the dazzlingly bright top light; the illustration on the wall is also used on the menu cover.

1/メインダイニング中央部の円形テーブルを見る 壁面のミラーが窓のような効果をあげている
2/トロピカルムードのバーコーナーをみる
3/バー 壁面の大きなミラーにもトロピカルなデザインがみられる
4/トップライトがまぶしいテラスダイニング 壁面のイラストはメニューの表紙にも使われている

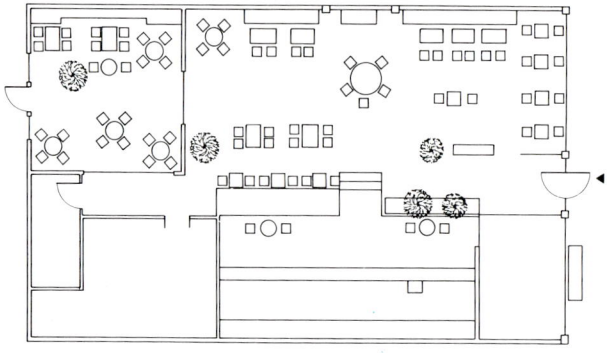

DON JOSE 〈Torrance, CA.〉

"DON JOSE" is a Mexican restaurant chain developing in California and Las Vegas. This restaurant in Torrance is composed of a restaurant space with 182 seats and a bar lounge with 200 seats having a disco floor. The bricked facade has a white wall, and the floor under a low ceiling is covered with patterned carpets, with accent on Mexican styled tiles and ceiling beams. Walls are decorated with Mexican handicrafts and stills of Western cowboy pictures, presenting an atmosphere of Mexican countryside. There are booth seating sections and small private rooms.
● DON JOSE (Torrance, CA.)
Address/21227 Hawthorne Boulevard Torrance, CA. 90503
Opened/June 1980;　Number of seats/382 (restaurant 182, bar lounge 200)

「ドン ホセ」は カリフォルニア州とラスベガスにチェーン展開しているメキシコ料理レストランである。トーランス店は 182席のレストランと200席のディスコフロアを持つバーラウンジで構成されている。煉瓦と白い壁のファサードで 天井の低い店内は 模様入りのカーペットが敷かれ メキシカン調のタイルや天井の梁がアクセントになっている。壁面には 民芸品や西部劇のスチール写真が飾られ メキシコの田舎風の造りになっている。レストランは ブース席とプライベート用の小部屋が用意されている。
●ドン ホセ〈カリフォルニア・トーランス〉
Address/21227 Hawthorne Boulevard Torrance. CA.90503　開店/1980年6月　客席数/382席(レストラン182席　バーラウンジ200席)

(Photo captions)
1 / The dance floor and bar corner.
2 / The guest seating area accented with an arch; the wall is decorated with Mexican handicrafts and stills of Western pictures.
3 / The entrance of the restaurant.

1/ダンスフロアとバーコーナー
2/アーチのある客席　壁面には民芸品や西部劇のスチール写真が飾られている
3/レストランへのエントランス

THE RED ONION ⟨Huntington Beach, CA.⟩

Since 1967 when the first Mexican restaurant opened near Los Angeles International Airport, "THE RED ONION" chain has developed mainly in California. "THE RED ONION Huntington Harbor" employs the traditional Spanish and the Mediterranean styles in its interior. The restaurant is on the 1st floor, while the 2nd floor is composed of a bar counter, lounge, table seating area where backgammon can be played, and dance floor.

● THE RED ONION
   (Huntington Beach, CA.)
Address/16450 Pacific Coast Highway Huntington Beach, CA. 92649
Opened/January 1980;   Number of seats/540 (restaurant 220, bar lounge 320)

「ザ レッドオニオン」は 1967年にロサンゼルス国際空港の近くに1号店をオープンし 以来カリフォルニアを中心にチェーン展開しているメキシコ料理レストラン。この「ハンティントン ハーバー店」は 伝統的なスペインと地中海風の様式を取り入れたインテリアで 1階はレストラン 2階がバーカウンターを中心に ラウンジやバックギャモンが出来るテーブル席とダンスフロアで構成されている。

●ザ レッドオニオン〈カリフォルニア・ハンティントン ビーチ〉
Address/16450 Pacific Coast Highway Huntington Beach, CA.92649 開店/1980年1月 客席数/540席(レストラン220席 バーラウンジ320席)

(Photo captions)
1 / The 1st floor dining area featuring the Mediterranean interior.
2 / The 2nd floor cocktail lounge has a gorgeous atmosphere.
3 / The 2nd floor cocktail lounge and dance floor.

1/地中海風インテリアの1階ダイニングエリア
2/2階カクテルラウンジはゴージャスな感じ
3/2階カクテルラウンジとダンスフロア

ACAPULCO Y LOS ARCOS ⟨Larkspur, CA.⟩

"ACAPULCO Y LOS ARCOS" is a Mexican style restaurant chain mainly developing in California. It is popular with Mexican style interior and spicy and voluminous but relatively cheap foods. This restaurant at Larkspur is situated about 10 miles to the north of San Francisco facing a high-class residential quarter, and intended for "young adults." Uniquely enough, the facade looks like a factory rather than a restaurant.

● ACAPULCO Y LOS ARCOS
 (Larkspur, CA.)
Address/Larkspur, CA.
Opened/June 1981;   Number of seats/300
(restaurant 200, bar 100)

「アカプルコ イ ロス アルコス」は カリフォルニア州を中心にチェーン展開するメキシカンスタイルのデザインと スパイシィでボリュームのあるメニューで比較的安い価格が魅力のレストラン。「ラークスパー店」は サンフランシスコの北約10マイルの地点の高級住宅地を背景とした立地で"ヤングアダルト"の客層をターゲットにしている。ファサードはレストランというよりは工場を思わせるユニークさだ。

●アカプルコ イ ロス アルコス⟨カリフォルニア・ラークスパー⟩
Address/Larkspur, CA.　開店/1981年6月　客席数/300席（レストラン200席　バー100席）

(Photo captions)
1 / The entrance hall; the reception and the bar corner behind.
2 / The bar lounge; features unique presentation of the tiled counter and waterfall.
3 / The dining area composed of Mexican style designs of wall illustration, beams and tiled floors.
4 / The facade.

1/エントランスホール　レセプションと後方はバーラウンジ
2/バーラウンジ　タイル貼りのカウンターや水を流し滝をイメージした演出がユニーク
3/壁面のイラストや梁　フロアのタイルなどメキシコ調のデザインで構成されたダイニングエリア
4/ファサード

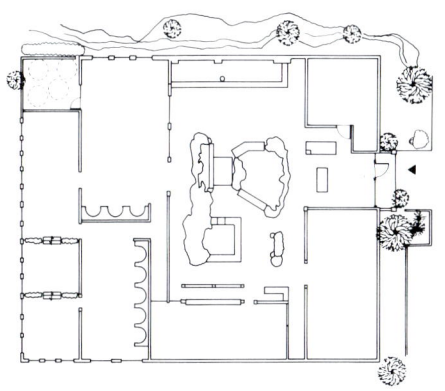

THE RED ONION ⟨Marina Del Rey, CA.⟩

Another Mexican restaurant in "THE RED ONION" chain opened on the beach area after "THE RED ONION Huntington Beach" (see page 38). "THE RED ONION Marina Del Rey" faces a yacht harbor, and although its interior design retains a vestige of Spanish and Mediterranean styles, it has a more casual atmosphere with playful and dream-like images.

● THE RED ONION (Marina Del Rey)
Address/4215 Admiralty Way Marina Del Rey, CA. 90291
Opened/February 1982; Number of seats/644 (restaurant 174, bar 100, nightclub 370)

「ハンティントン ビーチ店」(本書38ページ収録)に次いで 海岸地域に出店されたメキシカンレストラン。「マリナ デル レイ店」は ヨットハーバーに面して位置し デザインを伝統的なスペイン 地中海様式から その面影を残しながら よりカジュアルに変化させたのが特徴で 遊びの部分や夢をもたせた店のイメージを演出している。

● ザ レッド オニオン〈カリフォルニア・マリナデルレイ〉
Address/4215 Admiralty Way Marina Del Rey, CA.90291 開店/1982年2月 客席数/644席(レストラン174席 バー100席 ナイトクラブ370席)

(Photo captions)
1 / The bright, open dining and bar areas.
2 / The dining area effectively accented with green elements.
3 / Playful presentation with the ceiling-suspended objet display.

1/明るく開放的なダイニングとバーエリア
2/グリーンが効果的に配されたダイニングエリア
3/天井から吊り下げられたディスプレイにも遊び心が演出されている

CAFE BA·BA·REEBA! 〈Chicago〉

An orthdox tapas food restaurant in Chicago. "Tapas" is a type of food served on small plates which is often seen at taverns in Spain. Cooked mainly by using fish, chicken and eggs, tapas is usually taken as a side dish. 28 types of tapas are always on the menu, while about 10 types of specialty tapas are also served. The interior is full of Spanish mood — with cooking materials suspended from the ceiling, frescos painted by taking up Spanish images as a theme, and even employee uniform which is designed to stress Spanish atmosphere. Frequented by young professionals, artists, etc.
● CAFE BA·BA·REEBA! (Chicago)
Address/2024 N. Halsted Chicago, Illinois 60614
Phone/312-935-5000
Opened/December 1985; Number of seats/ 190 (plus 50 terrace seats in summer alone); Number of employees/98

シカゴにおける本格的タパス(tapas)料理のレストラン。スペインの居酒屋などでよく見られる小皿料理で 魚介類やチキン 卵など使ったいわばおつまみとして利用される。この店では常に28種類のタパス料理をメニューに掲げている。他にスペシャリティとして約10種類用意されている。店内は天井から食材がぶらさげられていたり スペインをテーマにした壁画があったり 従業員のユニフォームに至るまでスペインムードがあふれ ヤング プロフェッショナルや芸術家の好むレストランとして賑わっている。
●カフェ バ・バ・リーバ！〈シカゴ〉
Address/2024 N.Halsted Chicago,Illinois 60614
Phone/312-935-5000　開店/1985年12月　客席数/190席(別に夏季のみテラス50席使用)　従業員数/98人

(Photo captions)
1 / The dining room employs an atmosphere of Spanish tavern.
2 / The bar; accented with the paintings of Spanish scenery.
3 / Tapas cooking materials suspended from the ceiling and material showcase.

1/ダイニングルーム　スペインの居酒屋の雰囲気を取り入れている
2/バー　壁面にはスペインの風景が描かれている
3/天井から吊り下げられたタパス料理の食材とショーケース

KYOTARU ⟨Downey, CA.⟩

Opened by "KYOTARU" (headquartered in Tokyo), which is known for Edo taste and take-out sushi, this restaurant at Downey in the suburbs of Los Angeles is the first overseas pilot restaurant operating as a tenant of composite eating & drinking facility "Sanbi of Tokyo" which is run by a Japanese owner. Situated on a quarter where many middle-class people live, 90% of the restaurant's customers are Americans, while the rest are orientals including Japanese people. The interior is composed only of a counter with 19 seats, and customers to the annexed "Sanbi Restaurant" can also order sushi from the table seating area or bar corner where they are sitting. Just in front of the counter a huge 'kabuki' picture is displayed.

● KYOTARU (Downey, CA.)
Address/8649 Firestone Boulevard Downey, CA. 90241
Opened/April 1981; Number of seats/19 (counter seats alone); Number of employees/6

(Photo captions)
1 / The interior composed only of counter seats; decorated with a huge 'kabuki' picture.
2 / The entrance area viewed across vividly red napkins on the counter.

江戸前と持ち帰り寿司の「京樽」(本社・東京)の海外出店1号実験店として ロサンゼルス郊外のダウニー(Downey)の 日本人の経営する複合飲食施設「サンビ オブ トウキョウ」の一角にテナント出店したもの。中流階層の住民が多い場所に位置するこのレストランの利用客の90%はアメリカ人で 残りが日本人を含む東洋人という。店内は19席のカウンターだけで 併設された「サンビ レストラン」の各コーナーのテーブル席やバーからもオーダーできるようになっている。カウンター正面には大きな歌舞伎絵が飾られている。

●京樽〈カリフォルニア・ダウニー〉
Address/8649 Firestone Boulevard Downey,CA. 90241 開店/1981年4月 客席数/19席(カウンター席のみ) 従業員数/6人

1/カウンター席のみで構成された店内 大きな歌舞伎絵が飾られている
2/赤いナプキンが目立つカウンター越しに入口方向をみる

KISHO-AN ⟨Los Angeles⟩

①

②

A Japanese restaurant opened by "KISHO-AN" (headquartered in Kyoto) on the highest floor of high-class shopping center "Beverly Center" in Los Angeles. In addition to sushi and sashimi, the restaurant has developed new types of foods such as beef tempura and chicken tempura. Mainly intended for young people who are sensitive to fashion, the interior uses black as the basic tone accented with neon lighting, and waitresses wearing a blouse with a 'kabuki' picture are serving. It is said that the design, which has changed the image of Japanese restaurant, is the result of considerations given to the fact that the restaurant is in New York.

● KISHO-AN (Los Angeles)
Address/Beverly Center Top floor 131 N. La Cienega Boulevard Los Angeles, CA. 90044
Opened/October 1982; Number of seats/88 (table 70, counter 18); Number of employees/25

「吉祥庵」(本社・京都市)が ロサンゼルスの高級ショッピングセンター「ビバリーセンター」の最上階の飲食店街に出店。料理は寿司 刺身のほかに ビーフてんぷらやチキンてんぷらなどのメニューを開発している。ファッションに敏感な若者層にポイントを置き 黒を基調にした店づくりにネオンを導入 歌舞伎絵をあしらったブラウスを着たウェイトレスがサービスしている。この日本食レストランのイメージを変えたデザインは すべてニューヨークを意識したものという。

●吉祥庵〈ロサンゼルス〉
Address/Beverly Center Top floor 131 N.La Cienega Boulevard Los Angeles, CA.90044 開店/1982年10月 客席数/88席(テーブル70席 カウンター18席) 従業員数/25人

(Photo captions)
1 / The black-toned interior; with neon lighting also at the sushi counter.
2 / The facade; features a smartly designed menu.
3 / The wall is decorated with neoned menu items.

1/黒を基調にしたレストランの店内 寿司カウンターにもネオンを取り入れている
2/ファサード デザイン化されたメニューもポイントになっている
3/壁面にはメニューがネオンで表示されている

KANSAI SUSHI KAPPO ⟨Santa Monica, CA.⟩

In America, Japanese foods such as conventional specialty foods (e.g. sushi and tempura) have taken root, and even 'kaiseki' cuisine is appearing. Recently, "grazing" has become a fashionable eating style in which one can enjoy various types of food each in small portion. "KANSAI" was a restaurant exactly suitable for the new trend. The interior features a 'high tech' sense in white & black tone, cooks wearing a tie, and B.G.M. of fusion and jazz. The restaurant is closed now.

● KANSAI SUSHI KAPPO
(Santa Monica, CA.)
Closed now; Opened/March 1985; Number of seats/81 (table 70, sushi bar 15, 'Kappo' cuisine bar 6); Number of employees/21

日本食が定着したアメリカで 従来の寿司 てんぷらといった専門料理はもちろん 懐石料理まで出現している。1回の食事でいろいろな料理を少量ずつ楽しむグレージングのスタイルが流行し その新傾向にマッチさせたのがこの「カンサイ」である。店内は白と黒が基調のハイテック感覚であり 板前はネクタイを着用 B.G.M.はヒュージョンやジャズといった具合である。この店は現在閉店されている。

●カンサイ寿司割烹〈カリフォルニア・サンタモニカ〉
現在閉店中 開店/1985年3月 客席数/81席(テーブル70席 スシバー15席 割烹バー6席) 従業員数/21人

(Photo captions)
1 / The bright table seating area viewed across the long counter bar; through the large window one can see the courtyard.
2 / The table seating and counter seating areas in black & white tone.
3 / The table seating area; featuring a new-type interior design that stresses fashionableness.

1/長いカウンターバーを通して明るいテーブル席をみる 大きな窓からは中庭が眺められる
2/白と黒を基調にしたテーブル席とカウンター席
3/テーブル席 ファッション性で売る新しいタイプのデザイン

BENIHANA CAFE ⟨New York⟩

An experimental cafe-type restaurant opened in Manhattan by "BENIHANA OF TOKYO" (headquartered in Miami) which is developing a hot plate food restaurant chain throughout the U.S.A., "BENIHANA CAFE" features a light and casual food concept. By removing hot plate tables from the dining area, an open kitchen with a slender hot plate grill was installed in the center, coupled with a full-service dining room in white & black tone and a bar corner. The restaurant is closed now.
● BENIHANA CAFE (New York)
Closed now;　　Opened/March 23, 1990;
Number of seats/104 (dining 96, bar corner 8)

(Photo captions)
1 / The open kitchen with a hot plate grill; all cooking is performed here.
2・3 / The dining area in white & black tone.

全米に鉄板焼レストランを展開する「ベニハナ オブ トーキョー」(本社・マイアミ)が ライトでカジュアルなコンセプトを開発し マンハッタンに開店した実験店で カフェタイプのレストラン。ダイニングから鉄板焼のテーブルをなくし 細長い鉄板焼グリルを備えたオープンキッチンを中央に設け 白と黒を基調にしたフルサービスのダイニングルームとバーコーナーで構成している。この店は現在閉店している。
●ベニハナ カフェ〈ニューヨーク〉
現在閉店中　開店/1990年3月23日　客席数/104席(ダイニング96席　バーコーナー8席)

1・2/鉄板焼グリルがあるオープンキッチン　調理はすべてここで行われる
3/白と黒を基調にしたダイニング

CHINA CLUB ⟨Los Angeles⟩

A Chinese restaurant located against Beverly Hills and West Hollywood. Using a combined black & white tone as the design concept, the main dining area looks like an art gallery. The bar corner is accented with red stools which stand in contrast with the black counter. The terrace features tropical plants and the innermost tea house is decorated with Chinese characters which imply the four seasons.
45 types of new Chinese cuisine were served. The cooking materials were cut by Japanese, seasoned by Chinese and then dished up by French. "CHINA CLUB" used to be crowded with sophisticated artists, lawyers and those involved in films and music aged 25 to 45 years. To our regret, it is closed now.
● CHINA CLUB (Los Angeles)
Closed now; Opened/December 1980; Number of seats/150; Number of employees/30

(Photo captions)
1 / The main dining area viewed from the terrace dining area.
2 / The bar corner; with a top light above the counter.
3 / The main dining area; features an airbrushed impressive fresco of "celestial nymphs."

ビバリーヒルズとウエスト ハリウッドを背景にした立地の中国料理レストラン。黒と白を基本としたカラーコンセプトの店舗のデザインでアートギャラリー風のメインダイニング スツールに赤色を配し 黒のカウンターとコントラストを持たせたバーコーナー トロピカルなプリントを持ち込んだテラスダイニング 四季をテーマにした中国文字をデザインした最奥部のティーハウスなどで構成されている。料理は新しい中国料理45品を提供。調理には日本人が食材のカットをし 中国人が味付けし フランス人が盛り付ける方法をとっている。店舗や料理サービスにテイストやスタイルが感じられるこのレストランは ソフィストケートされた25〜45才を中心としたアーティストや弁護士 映画や音楽関係の客で賑わっていたが 残念ながら現在は閉店されている。
● チャイナ クラブ ⟨ロサンゼルス⟩
現在閉店中　開店/1980年12月　客席数/150席　従業員数/30人

1/テラスダイニングからメインダイニングをみる
2/バーコーナー　カウンターの上部にトップライトが設けられている
3/"天女"がテーマのエアブラシによる壁画が印象的なメインダイニング

AKASAKA HANTEN ⟨Los Angeles⟩

A high-class Chinese restaurant opened in the shopping center "Weller Court" in Little Tokyo, Los Angeles. Getting out of conventional Chinese image, the interior design incorporates modern elements such as brass pipes conveying the image of bamboo, partition looking like a 'shoji' (paper sliding screen), wall on which bamboos are designed against the silver background, and fan-shaped lighting. "AKASAKA HANTEN" offers a wide variety of foods ranging from Canton dish to Peking dish which mainly uses Peking duck, prawn and crab, Sichuan and even Shanghai cuisine. Mainly used by 2nd/3rd generation (nisei/sansei) Japanese-Americans, Japanese representatives residing in America, U.S. government officers, lawyers and other high-class people, as well as by tourists from Japan.

● AKASAKA HANTEN (Los Angeles)
Address/123 S. Weller Street 2nd floor, Los Angeles, CA. 90012
Opened/November 1980; Number of seats/198; Number of employees/30

ロサンゼルスのリトルトウキョウのショッピングセンター「ウエラー コート（Weller Court）」に出店した高級中国料理レストラン。インテリアは旧来のチャイニーズ イメージを脱し 真鍮のパイプで表現された竹 障子を思わせるパーティション シルバーの地に竹をデザインした壁面 団扇で構成された照明など モダンなタッチになっている。料理は広東料理とペキンダック エビ カニ料理をメインにした北京 そして四川 上海料理と幅広い。客層は日系の2～3世や駐在員 アメリカの政府関係者や弁護士などハイクラスの人たちや日本からの旅行者など。

●赤坂飯店〈ロサンゼルス〉
Address/123 S.Weller Street 2nd floor, Los Angeles, CA.90012 開店/1980年11月 客席数/198席 従業員数/30人

(Photo captions)
1 / The dining room divided by the partition which looks like a 'shoji.'
2 / The aisle with hanging scrolls; the wall design images bamboos.
3 / The dining area decorated with brass pipes imaging bamboos and fan-shaped lighting.

1/障子をイメージしたパーティションで仕切られたダイニングルーム
2/通路に掛け軸が飾られている 壁面には竹のイメージをデザインしている
3/竹を表現した真鍮のパイプと団扇をデザインした照明器具があるダイニングエリア

③

FRAGRANT VEGETABLE RESTAURANT ⟨Los Angeles⟩

A Chinese restaurant which uses only vegetables as materials — gluten instead of pork, bean curd 'tofu' instead of beef, and mushroom instead of abalone and shrimps, for instance. Chemical seasonings are not used at all, while only corn oil is used. Thus, the menu is thoroughly health-oriented, but foods taste like those cooked by using meat and fish. Based on 'shojin' dishes handed down from the Indian Buddhism, the restaurant has succeeded in developing their own originals.
The interior is decorated with paintings which express the world of Buddhism and Buddhist images. However, it does not give a religious impression, but looks very bright so that the healthy sense is stressed.
● FRAGRANT VEGETABLE
   RESTAURANT (Los Angeles)
Address/11859 Wilshire Boulevard
Los Angeles, CA. 90025
Phone/213-312-1442
Opened/November 1987; Number of seats/120; Number of employees/11

使用食材は野菜だけというチャイニーズレストラン。豚肉のかわりにグルテン 牛肉は豆腐 あわびやエビはマッシュルームで作る。化学調味料はまったく使わず 油もコーンオイルだけと 徹底したヘルシーコンセプトで しかも味は肉や魚介類を使用したものと変わらない。インド仏教伝来の精神料理に由来し 独自の研究から生み出されたものという。店内には仏教の世界を表現した絵や仏像が飾られているが 宗教的な感じはなく 明るい店づくりがヘルシー感覚をより強調している。
●香齋厨〈ロサンゼルス〉
Address/11859 Wilshire Boulevard Los Angeles, CA.90025 Phone/213-312-1442 開店/1987年11月 客席/120席 従業員数/11人

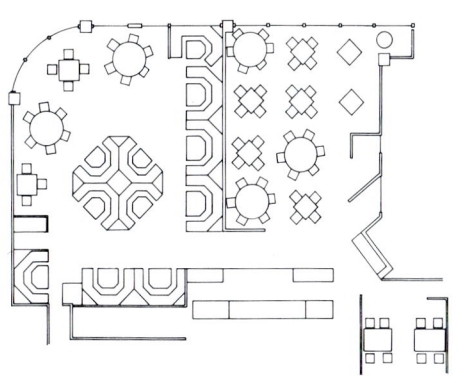

(Photo captions)
1 / The cut glass with a lotus flower design, and the bright, elegant table seating corner.
2 / The bright interior decorated with paintings related to Buddhism.
3 / The restaurant on the 1st floor of a building facing Wilshire Blvd.

1/蓮の花がデザインされたカットグラスと明るくエレガントな感じのテーブル席
2/仏教に関した絵が飾られた明るい店内
3/ウイルシャー通りに面したビルの1階にあるレストラン

CHOPSTIX ⟨Los Angeles⟩

Using a parody of "Chopsticks," "CHOPSTIX" is a dim sum cafe situated on Melrose Avenue where there are many boutiques, antique shops, restaurants, etc. Here, vegetables, fish, chicken and other ingredients are cooked in Chinese or Thai style without using chemical seasonings and artificial coloring at all. A gas station built in the 1920s was redecorated, but an art deco tower on the roof, which has not been removed, serves as a landmark. The contemporary interior is composed of the counter and table seating area with high chairs, with emphasis on cleanness. Guests can enjoy watching dim dum, such as fried dumplings stuffed with minced pork, being cooked at the open kitchen.

● CHOPSTIX (Los Angeles)
Address/7229 Melrose Avenue Los Angeles, CA. 90046
Phone/213-937-1111
Opened/February 1988; Number of seats/85 (counter 20, table 35, patio 30); Number of employees/53

(Photo captions)
1 / The facade facing Melrose Avenue; a gas station was redecorated.
2 / The contemporary and bright interior.
3 / The fanciful toilet presentation; with tropical fish swimming in the wall space.
4 / Popular dishes such as chicken salads, fried rice and dim sum.

店名は"Chopsticks＝箸"のもじりで ブティックやアンティークショップ レストランなどが集まるメルロース アベニューに立地するディムサム カフェ。料理は野菜類 魚 チキンなどの食材を化学調味料や人工の香料 着色料などを使用せずに 中国風 タイ風に調理し提供している。建物は1920年代に建てられたガソリンスタンドを改装したもので 屋根にはアートデコのタワーがそのまま残され ランドマークとなる外観になっている。コンテンポラリーなつくりの店内は カウンターとハイチェアのテーブル席で構成され 清潔さを強調し オープンキッチンを備え 餃子 包子類(Dim Sum)を作る様を客に見せている。

1/メルロース アベニューに面したレストランのファサード ガソリンスタンドを改装したもの
2/コンテンポラリーで明るい店内
3/トイレの壁面の熱帯魚を泳がせた演出が奇抜
4/チキンサラダやフライドライス ディムサムなどの人気料理

●チョップスティックス〈ロサンゼルス〉
Address/7229 Melrose Avenue Los Angeles, CA.90046 Phone/213-937-1111 開店/1988年2月 客席数/85席(カウンター20席 テーブル35席 パティオ30席) 従業員数/53人

イタリア料理レストラン

アロ アロ〈ニューヨーク〉 64
レミ〈ニューヨーク〉 66
バリオ〈ニューヨーク〉 68
トラットリア デル アルテ〈ニューヨーク〉 70
マルヴァシア〈ニューヨーク〉 72
ティーディーエル フードショー〈カリフォルニア・ビバリーヒルズ〉 74
フージ〈ニューヨーク〉 76
スクージ〈シカゴ〉 78
ピナフィーニ〈ロサンゼルス〉 80
ル マドリ〈ニューヨーク〉 82
ビーチェ〈ニューヨーク〉 84
イル フォナイオ "ガストロノミア イタリアーナ"
〈サンフランシスコ〉 86
カーディーニ〈ロサンゼルス〉 88
コリンティア〈サンフランシスコ〉 90
ジ オールド スパゲティ ファクトリー
〈カリフォルニア・ハリウッド〉 92

Italian restaurants

ALO ALO ⟨New York⟩ 64
REMI ⟨New York⟩ 66
PALIO ⟨New York⟩ 68
TRATTORIA DELL' ARTE ⟨New York⟩ 70
MALVASIA ⟨New York⟩ 72
DDL FOODSHOW ⟨Beverly Hills, CA.⟩ 74
SFUZZI ⟨New York⟩ 76
SCOOZI ⟨Chicago⟩ 78
PINAFINI ⟨Los Angeles⟩ 80
LE MADRI ⟨New York⟩ 82
BICE ⟨New York⟩ 84
IL FORNAIO "GASTRONOMIA ITALIANA" ⟨San Francisco⟩ 86
CARDINI ⟨Los Angeles⟩ 88
CORINTIA ⟨San Francisco⟩ 90
THE OLD SPAGHETTI FACTORY ⟨Hollywood, CA.⟩ 92

ALO ALO 〈New York〉

"Alo Alo" occupies part of "Trump Plaza" which is composed of high class residences and specialty stores, facing the crossing of the East Side 61 Street and the 3rd Avenue. It forms a box-shaped space 40 feet in height and about the same in width with glazed walls on three sides. In order to cover the high ceiling, illuminators are suspended from the ceiling in various lengths. Life-size waiter and waitress objets are placed on the pastel-colored walls where woods are painted, thereby accentuating the interior with ironical and humorous presentation. The name "Alo Alo" is Portuguese, meaning "Hello Hello" as half joking. Mainly serving North Italian cuisine, it is a fashionable restaurant frequented by young professionals, entertainers and people involved in fashion.

● ALO ALO (New York)
Address/1030 3rd Avenue 61st Street & 3rd Avenue New York, N.Y. 10021
Phone/212-838-4343
Opened/March 1985; Number of seats/120; Number of employees/50

「アロ アロ」は イーストサイドの61丁目(61 Street)と3番街(3rd Avenue)のコーナーにある高級住宅と専門店で構成された「トランプ プラザ」の一角に位置する。三方がガラスで囲まれたこのレストランは 40フィートの高さの天井と ほぼ同じ幅を持つボックス状の店で 高い天井をカバーするために様々な高さで照明を吊り下げている。パステル調の色で描かれた壁面の森の絵の中に 等身大のウェイターやウェイトレスのオブジェを置き 風刺とユーモアを演出した店づくりにしている。店名はポルトガル語で ジョークをこめた"ハロー ハロー"の意味。北イタリア地方の料理がメインで 若いプロフェッショナルや芸能人 ファッション関係の人たちがあつまるファッショナブルなレストランである。

●アロ アロ 〈ニューヨーク〉
Address/1030 3rd Avenue 61st Street & 3rd Avenue New York, N.Y.10021 Phone/212-838-4343 開店/1985年3月 客席数/120席 従業員数/50人

(Photo captions)
1/The entrance area and bar corner viewed from an inner part.
2/The dining area accented with the humorous life-size objets.
3/The reception viewed from the bar corner.
4/The box-like facade with glazed walls on three sides, facing the crossing of the 3rd Avenue and 61 Street.

1/店内奥からエントランス方向とバーコーナーをみる
2/ユーモアのある等身大のオブジェが置かれたダイニングエリア
3/バーコーナーからレセプションをみる
4/3番街と61丁目の角に面し 三方をガラスに囲まれたボックス状のファサード

②

③

REMI 〈New York〉

An Italian restaurant designed, produced and managed by designer Adam D. Tihany himself. The menu is composed of 37 types of antipasto, fish, pasta, meat and other dishes. The name "Remi" means an oar of gondola, and on the walls Venetian scenes are painted (by Paulin Paris). The table seating area is presented at a level of gondola from which guests look up at canal bridge girders and Venetian scenery.

● REMI (New York)
Address/145 West 53rd Street New York, N.Y. 10019
Phone/212-581-4242
Opened/June 11, 1990; Number of seats/240 (dining 160, terrace 70, bar 10);

デザイナー・アダム ティハニー(Adam D. Tihany)が設計プロデュースし 自らが経営するイタリア料理レストラン。アンティパスト 魚 パスタ 肉料理など 37種類のディナーメニューで構成されている。「REMI」とはゴンドラのオールのことで 壁面にはヴェニスの風景が描かれている。ポウリン パリ(Paulin Paris)の作品。テーブル席はゴンドラに乗った位置であり 上方に運河の橋桁とヴェニスの風景が見えるといった演出である。

●レミ〈ニューヨーク〉
Address/145 West 53rd Street New York, N.Y.10019 Phone/212-581-4242 開店/1990年6月11日 客席数/240席(ダイニング160席 テラス70席 バー10席)

(Photo captions)
1 / The interior presenting Venetian scenery; the fresco, painted by Paulin Paris, extends for about 36 m long and in 120 degrees; the table seating area is presented at a level of gondola from which guests look up at canal bridge girders and Venetian scenery.
2 / The spacious reception area.
3 / The bar area; provided with Venetian chandeliers and Murano glassware in the 18th century.

1/ヴェニスの風景を演出した店内 幅約36m 120度に展開するポウリン パリの壁画 テーブル席はゴンドラに乗った位置で 上方に運河の橋桁とヴェニスの風景が見えるといった演出
2/広い空間をもつレセプション廻り
3/バーエリア ベネチアン シャンデリアや 18世紀のムラノグラス(Murano glassware)を配している

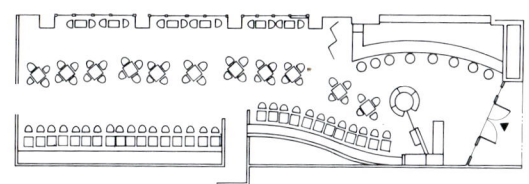

PALIO 〈New York〉

An Italian restaurant occupying the 1st and 2nd floors of the Equitable Center which stands on West 51 St., New York. Managed by Mr. Tomy May. The chef Andreda Merano offers cuisine which agrees well with the present American life style. The shop design is undertaken by Massimo Vignelli. A bar is on the 1st floor and a restaurant on the 2nd floor. The bar is composed of a counter and table seating area; accented with a fresco of a horse race event scene in Palio (which was employed as the shop name) district, Italy, painted (by Sandro Chia) over the upper part of the wall, giving a dramatic impression. Featuring a gray-toned composed atmosphere, the dining area is partitioned into three sections by wine racks.
- PALIO (New York)
Address/151 West 51st Street New York, N.Y. 10019
Phone/212-245-4850
Opened/August 1987; Number of seats/217 (restaurant 125, bar 52, two private rooms 40); Number of employees/90〜100

①

ニューヨークの西51丁目のEquitable Centerの1〜2階にあるイタリア料理レストラン。経営はTomy May氏。シェフのAndreda Merano氏は 現在のアメリカ人のライフスタイルに合った料理を提供している。デザインはMassimo Vignelli氏。1階はバー 2階がレストランで バーはカウンターとテーブル席で構成され 壁面上部に描かれた店名にもなっている。イタリア パリオ地方の競馬のイベント風景の壁画(Sandro Chia氏作)が圧巻。ダイニングは 茶色を基調とした落ち着いた雰囲気で ワインラックで3つのセクションに分けられている。
●パリオ 〈ニューヨーク〉
Address/151 West 51st Street New York, N.Y. 10019 Phone/212-245-4850 開店/1987年8月 客席数/217席(レストラン125席 バー52席 個室 2室/40席) 従業員数/90〜100人

②

③

(Photo captions)
1 / The 2nd floor dining area; partitioned into three sections by wine racks.
2 / The table setting.
3・4 / The 1st floor bar corner; the counter is finished with marble; the fresco fully painted over the upper part of the wall gives a dramatic impression.

1/2階ダイニングエリア ワインラックで3つのセクションにしきられている
2/テーブルセッティング
3・4/1階バーコーナー カウンターはマーブル 上部壁面いっぱいに描かれた壁画が圧巻

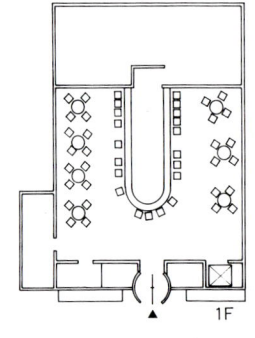
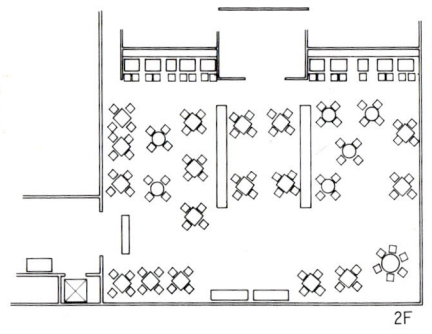

TRATTORIA DELL'ARTE ⟨New York⟩

Designed by Milton Glaser, "Trattoria Dell'-Arte" means an "Italian restaurant with fine arts." The interior is decorated with large objets of body parts, such as ears, lips and breasts on the wall. On the 1st floor there are a bar and three dining rooms, while the 2nd floor has rooms which can be used for private parties. The menu includes 20 types of cold and hot hors d'œuvre, and other basic Italian foods such as pizza, pasta, fish and charcoaled veal.

● TRATTORIA DELL'ARTE (New York)
Address/900 7th Avenue at 57th Street New York, N.Y. 10019
Phone/212-245-9800
Opened/October 1988;   Number of seats/280

(Photo captions)
1 / The colorful and bright dining room; with the wall design composed of partial sketches and objets of human body which remind us of Leonardo da Vinci.
2・3 / The wall is decorated with objets of ears, lips, breasts, etc.
4 / The 2nd floor room used for wine tasting and private dining.
5 / The facade features an impressive objet of Italian big nose.

1/カラフルで明るいダイニングルーム　レオナルド ダ ヴィンチを連想させるスケッチやオブジェで デザイン構成されている
2・3/壁面には耳　唇　乳房などのオブジェが飾られている
4/2階のワイン テイスティングとプライベート ダイニングに使用される部屋
5/ファサード　イタリア人の大きな鼻が目立つ

"美術のイタリアン レストラン"とうたった「トラットリア デルアルテ」は ミルトン グレイザー(Milton Glaser)がデザインした店。店内には耳　唇　乳房などのオブジェが壁面に飾られている。1階にはバーと3つのダイニングルーム　2階にはプライベート パーティ用の部屋が用意されている。20種類の冷製と温製のオードブル ピザ パスタ 魚 仔牛肉の炭焼きなど ベーシックなイタリア料理を提供している。

●トラットリア デルアルテ〈ニューヨーク〉
Address/900 7th Avenue at 57th Street New York, N.Y.10019　Phone/212-245-9800　開店/1988年10月　客席数/280席

②

③

④

⑤

MALVASIA 〈New York〉

"Malvasia" was named after a dessert wine produced in Lipari Island, South Italy, from which the owner-chef Gennaro Picone came. Imaging the waves of the Mediterranean Sea, the interior was designed by Adam Tihany who has combined Greek, African and Italian designs. Foods served here are unique mixtures of Italian and Mediterranean foods which are simply but savorily seasoned.

● MALVASIA (New York)
Address/185 East 60th Street New York, N.Y. 10022
Phone/212-223-4790
Opened/May 16, 1989; Number of seats/80

店名の「マルヴァシア」は シェフでオーナーのジェナーロ ピコネ (Gennaro Picone) の出身地である南イタリアのリパリ (Lipari) 島のデザートワインに由来している。店づくりは地中海の波をテーマに ギリシャ アフリカ イタリアなどのデザインを組みあわせている。設計はアダム ティハニーで 料理はイタリアと地中海料理をミックスした独特なもので シンプルだが強くコクのある味付けが特色。
●マルヴァシア〈ニューヨーク〉
Address/185 East 60th Street New York, N.Y. 10022　Phone/212-223-4790　開店/1989年5月16日　客席数/80席

(Photo captions)
1 / The interior presentation expressing the nocturnal light, waves, etc. on the Mediterranean Sea. Looking up at the ceiling high above the bar counter, one finds an iron & copper chandelier designed by Adam D. Tihany.
2 / Overlooking the bar area from the 2nd floor; decorated by using blue, terra-cotta, beige, etc. as the theme colors.
3 / The entrance area viewed from an inner part of the 1st floor dining area; the interior is a mixture of Greek, African and Italian designs.
4 / The facade designs an image of waves.

1/地中海の夜 光 波などを表現した店内の演出 バーカウンターの上方の天井には アダム ティハニー (Adam D.Tihany) がデザインしたシャンデリアがある
2/2階からバーエリアを見下ろす テーマカラーはブルー テラコッタ ベージュなど
3/1階ダイニングの奥から入口方向をみる ギリシャ アフリカ イタリアなどのデザインがミックスされた店づくり
4/波のイメージをデザインしたファサード

DDL FOODSHOW ⟨Beverly Hills, CA.⟩

An Italian restaurant opened by film producer Dino De Laurentiis at Beverly Drive Street where high-class boutiques stand in a row. The 1st floor was used as a dining area with a food shop annexed to it, and the 2nd floor was used for a kitchen. Since movie lights are suspended from the ceiling with a deep stairwell, we felt as if in a studio. The wall surfaces were fully decorated with movie poster panels, and the bright, open interior atmosphere was very popular. At present, however, it is closed.

● DDL FOODSHOW (Beverly Hills, CA.)
Closed now;　　Opened/November 1984;
Number of seats/90

映画プロデューサー・ディノ デ ロレンディス（Dino De Laurentiis）氏が　高級ブティックが建ち並ぶビバリー ドライブ（Beverly Drive）に開店したイタリアンレストラン。1階はフードショップを併設したダイニングエリアで　2階はキッチンになっている。吹き抜けの高い天井からは撮影用のライトが吊り下げられ　映画のスタジオの雰囲気を醸しだしている。壁面には映画のポスターパネルが飾られ　開放的で明るい店内は好評だったが　現在は閉店されている。

●ディーディーエル フードショー⟨カリフォルニア・ビバリーヒルズ⟩
現在閉店中　開店/1984年11月　客席数/90席

(Photo captions)
1 / The wall surfaces decorated with movie poster panels.
2 / The restaurant reminding us of a movie studio; the food shop is attached.
3 / The facade facing the Beverly Drive.

②

1/壁面には映画のポスターパネルが飾られている
2/映画のスタジオを思わせるレストラン フードショップも併設している
3/ビバリー ドライブに面したファサード

③

SFUZZI ⟨New York⟩

"Sfuzzi" is an upscale Italian restaurant whose first chain restaurant opened in 1987 in Dallas. "Sfuzzi" is an Italian slang meaning "pleasant cuisine," and was designed by imaging the Mediterranean remains. The menu includes 9 types of hors d'œuvre, 5 types of pizza, 6 types of pasta, 7 types of speciality (fish, chicken, meat, etc.), and 4 types of side order. The speciality menu is common to all chain restaurants so that one can enjoy eating the same quality of foods everywhere in the chain.

● SFUZZI (New York)
Address/53 West 65th Street New York, N.Y. 10023
Phone/212-873-3700
Opened/May 1988;   Number of seats/160;
Number of employees/85

1987年にダラスに1号店を開店し チェーン展開しているアップスケールなイタリアンレストラン。店名はイタリア語のスラングで"楽しい料理"の意味。デザインは地中海地方の遺跡がテーマ。メニューは前菜が9種 ピザが5種 パスタが6種 魚 チキン 肉料理など スペシャリティが7種 サイドオーダーが4種などで構成。スペシャリティはユニフォーム メニューを採用し どの店へ行っても同じクォリティで同じ味の料理が食べられるのが特徴。

●フージ ⟨ニューヨーク⟩
Address/53 West 65th Street New York, N.Y. 10023 Phone/212-873-3700　開店/1988年5月　客席数/160席　従業員数/85席

①

②

(Photo captions)
1 / The dining area facing the West 65th Street; designed by imaging the Mediterranean remains with columns.
2 / The bar corner.
3 / The white table seating area which stands out against the columns and bricked walls; the wine cellar is visible in the center.

1/西65丁目通り(West 65th Street)に面したダイニングエリア　円柱があり地中海地方の遺跡をイメージしたデザイン
2/バーコーナー
3/円柱やレンガの壁に一際目立つ白いテーブル席　中央にはワインセラーがみえる

SCOOZI ⟨Chicago⟩

Pursuing an image of Italian rustic restaurant, "Scoozi" opened by redecorating a garage at a corner of a downtown warehouse. The interior is deliberately finished to look old and produce an Italian atmosphere. The wall has parts that have come off, and the inner brick surface is exposed, thus endeavoring to present "oldness." By using wooden beams beneath the arched ceiling, the wide interior space is designed to give an unobstructed view without pillars. Operated only for dinner, this restaurant is favored by many young professionals and ladies.

● SCOOZI (Chicago)
Address/410 West Huron Street Chicago, Illinois 60610
Phone/312-943-5900
Opened/December 1986; Number of seats/325; Number of employees/150

(Photo captions)
1・2 / The dining area; designed to give an old Italian atmosphere with the arched beams, mosaic floor and wall.
3 / The bar corner.
4 / The facade uniquely accented with a large tomato objet.

1・2/ダイニングエリア アーチ状の梁 モザイク状の床 壁面など オールド イタリアンをイメージしたデザイン
3/バーコーナー
4/入口に大きなトマトがあるユニークなファサード

イタリアの田舎風レストランをテーマにした「スクージ」は ダウンタウンの倉庫街の一角のガレージを改装してオープンした。店内はオールド イタリアンの雰囲気を出すために意識的に古く見せている。壁面には 薄く剝がれた部分があり その下から煉瓦のブリックがのぞいていたり 古さを演出している。アーチ状の天井に木の梁を設け 広い店内には柱を使わず見通しのよい空間構成にしている。ディナーのみの営業で 若いプロフェッショナルや女性客の利用が多い。

● スクージ ⟨シカゴ⟩
Address/410 West Huron Street Chicago, Illinois 60610　Phone/312-943-5900　開店/1986年12月　客席数/325席　従業員数/150人

PINAFINI ⟨Los Angeles⟩

An Italian restaurant on the 1st floor of high-class shopping center "Beverly Center," "Pinafini" was adjacent to "Hard Rock Cafe" (see page 152) where young people gathered. White and red are the theme colors of "Pinafini"; the ceiling, walls, floor and even tables are in white, while red is used on stools, napkins and the ceiling above the bar counter, thus creating a 'high tech' sense. At present, however, it is closed.
● PINAFINI (Los Angeles)
Closed now;   Opened/April 1985;   Number of seats/190;   Number of employees/46

高級ショッピングセンター「ビバリー センター (Beverly Center)」の1階にあるイタリアンレストランで 「ハード ロック カフェ (Hard Rock Cafe)」(本書152ページ収録)の隣り 若者たちが集まる場所に位置している。「ピナフィーニ」のテーマカラーは白と赤で 店内は天井 壁 床 テーブルを白で統一し スツールとナプキン バーカウンターの天井部に赤を使用し ハイテック感覚のデザインでまとめている。このレストランは現在閉店されている。
●ピナフィーニ〈ロサンゼルス〉
現在閉店中　開店/1985年4月　客席数/190席　従業員数/46人

1・2/バーコーナー　白いタイル貼りのカウンターとフロアにハイテックなデザインの天井 ブルーとピンクのネオンがアクセントをつけている
3/レセプションとダイニングコーナー

(Photo captions)
1・2 / The bar corner; the white tiled counter and floor versus the ceiling designed with a 'high tech' sense, accented with the blue and pink neons.
3 / The reception and dining corner.

LE MADRI 〈New York〉

Opened by Mr. Pino Luongo in Chelsea, "LE MADRI" is an Italian restaurant serving Tuscan foods. In the spacious dining room in the Renaissance style, one finds a service station decorated with colorful antipasto plates which are filled with fresh vegetables, sausages and cheese. A pizza oven using firewood is also installed to serve pizzas and very popular warm salads at midnight.

● LE MADRI (New York)
Address/168 West 18th Street New York, N.Y. 10011
Phone/212-727-8022
Opened/May 1989;   Number of seats/145;
Number of employees/90

ピノ ルオンゴ(Pino Luongo)氏がチェルシー(Chelsea)地区にオープンした イタリアのタスカン(Tuscan)地方料理のレストラン。ルネッサンス スタイルの広々としたダイニングルームには 新鮮な野菜やソーセージ チーズなどの食材に囲まれ カラフルなアンティパストの皿を飾ったサービス ステーションがある。薪を燃やすピザオーブンも設けられ 深夜にはピザと評判の温かいサラダがサービスされる。

●ル マドリ〈ニューヨーク〉
Address/168 West 18th Street New York, N.Y. 10011 Phone/212-727-8022 開店/1989年5月
客席数/145席 従業員数/90人

(Photo captions)
1 / The service bar and pizza oven.
2 / The appearance looks like a château. A dining room is installed on the 1st floor of the adjacent brick building.
3 / The white stucco walled dining room; accented with indirect lighting.

1/サービスバーとピザオーブン
2/シャトーを思わせるキッチンの外観 隣接する煉瓦の建物の1階がダイニングルームになっている
3/白いスタッコ壁のダイニングルーム 間接照明でアクセントされている

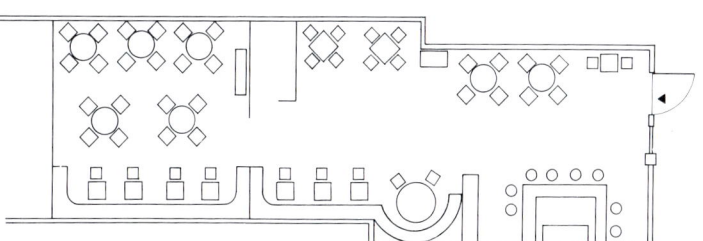

BICE 〈New York〉

An orthodox north Italian restaurant which opened in Milano in 1926. "BICE" in New York has a composed atmosphere with its almost pillar-free, spacious interior which features white cloth tables and large wood chairs in rows under indirect lighting. Designed by Adam D. Tihany.

● BICE (New York)
Address/7 East 54th Street New York, N.Y. 10022
Phone/212-688-1999
Opened/July 7, 1987; Number of seats/169 (dining 154, bar 15)

ミラノに 1926年にオープンした「ビーチェ」は 本格的な北イタリア料理レストラン。このニューヨーク店は ほとんど柱を感じさせない広々とした店内に 間接光に照らされた白いクロスのテーブルと大きな木製の椅子が並べられ落ち着いた雰囲気の店づくりになっている。デザインはアダム ティハニー。

●ビーチェ〈ニューヨーク〉
Address/7 East 54th Street New York, N.Y. 10022 Phone/212-688-1999 開店/1987年7月7日 客席数/169席(ダイニング154席 バー15席)

①

②

③

(Photo captions)
1 / The facade has an impressive logo inscribed with "1926" when "BICE" was founded.
2 / The uniquely designed bench seating area in the center.
3 / The curved bar counter.
4 / The uniquely designed ceiling of 154-seated dining room under indirect lighting.

1/ファサード 創業の1926年の文字があるロゴが目立つ
2/店内中央にはユニークなデザインのベンチ席がある
3/曲線を持たせたバーカウンター
4/ユニークな天井デザイン 間接光の下に154席のダイニングが広がる

IL FORNAIO "GASTRONOMIA ITALIANA" ⟨San Francisco⟩

A bakery & cafe style restaurant opened by Il Fornaio America Corporation, tying up with Il Fornaio which is developing a chain in Europe centering around Italy. The interior is composed of a takeout corner, bakery corner, bar, dining area, terrace dining area, etc. The interior is in Tuscan (midwestern Italian) style, while the food is Trattorian (north Italian), and can be tasted in a casual atmosphere.

● IL FORNAIO
"GASTRONOMIA ITALIANA"
(San Francisco)
Address/Levis Plaza, 1265 Battery Street San Francisco, CA. 94111
Phone/415-986-0100
Opened/November 1988; Number of seats/ 244 (restaurant 170, bar 30, terrace dining 44); Number of employees/85

イタリアを中心にヨーロッパにチェーン展開しているベーカリーチェーン Il Fornaioと提携し Il Fornaio America Corporationがオープンしたベーカリーとカフェスタイルのレストラン。店内はテイクアウトコーナー ベーカリーコーナー バー ダイニングエリアとテラスダイニングなどで構成されている。インテリアはイタリア中世部のタスカン(Tuscan)スタイルで料理は気取らない北イタリアのトラットリアスタイル。

●イル フォナイオ "ガストロノミア イタリアーナ"〈サンフランシスコ〉
Address/Levis Plaza, 1265 Battery Street San Francisco, CA.94111 Phone/415-986-0100
開店/1988年11月 客席数/244席(レストラン170席 バー30席 テラスダイニング44席) 従業員数/85人

(Photo captions)
1 / The outside light comes in the dining room having an open atmosphere under the high ceiling.
2 / The dining area composed of interior, frescos, etc. in Tuscany, midwestern Italy.
3 / The round table seating area; the interior has a number of corners which distinctively differ in atmosphere.
4 / The neat facade and entrance stand in sharp contrast to the interior.

1/高い天井のダイニングには外光がさしこみ 開放的な雰囲気
2/イタリア中西部のタスカン(Tuscan)地方のインテリアやフラスコ画で構成されたダイニングエリア
3/円形に並べられたテーブル席 店内はそれぞれ雰囲気を変えたいくつかのコーナーで構成されている
4/ファサードやエントランスは店内とは対象的にこじんまりしている

CARDINI 〈Los Angeles〉

Situated in "Hilton Hotel" downtown Los Angeles, "CARDINI" is a restaurant taking up north Italy as its theme. The menu is composed of fresh & light Italian cuisine cooked by the chef Ruggero Gadali. Inside the restaurant, 5,000 sq. ft. wide, there are six large pillars which are skillfully utilized to express an Italian street scene. The main street is expressed by a marble floor from the entrance to the inner part. The left side is used for a kitchen area, while the right side is composed of six rooms as the dining and bar space. Alleys are secured between the rooms so that they are used as an employees' service aisle.

● CARDINI (Los Angeles)
Address/Los Angeles Hilton Hotel, 930 Wilshire Boulevard Los Angeles, CA. 90017 Phone/213-629-4321 (3550)
Opened/November 1985; Number of seats/220 (inside 136, patio 84)

(Photo captions)
1 / The facade of the restaurant in "Hilton Hotel"; takes up an Italian street scene as the design theme.
2 / The entrance hall finished with marble expresses the main street.
3 / The dining room; toned in pale blue and grey, the interior expresses the sunset in winter.

1/ホテル内のレストランのファサード イタリアの街並みをデザインのテーマにしている
2/大理石貼りのエントランスホールは 街のメインストリートを表現している
3/ダイニングルーム 淡いブルーとグレーの色調で表現された冬のサンセットの雰囲気

ロサンゼルスのダウンタウンの「ヒルトンホテル」にある 北イタリアをテーマにしたレストラン。メニューはフレッシュ＆ライトイタリアンで シェフはRuggero Gadali氏。5,000平方フィートの店内には 6本の大きな柱がありこれを活かしてイタリアの街並みを表現している。メインストリートは入口から奥までの大理石のフロアで その左側はキッチンエリア 右側と奥はダイニングとバーの6つの部屋で構成されている。各部屋の間にはアリィ（裏通り）を設けて 従業員のサービス通路にしている。

●カーディーニ〈ロサンゼルス〉
Address/Los Angeles Hilton Hotel, 930 Wllshire Boulevard Los Angeles, CA.90017 Phone/213-629-4321(3550) 開店/1985年11月 客席数/336席(室内136席 パティオ84席)

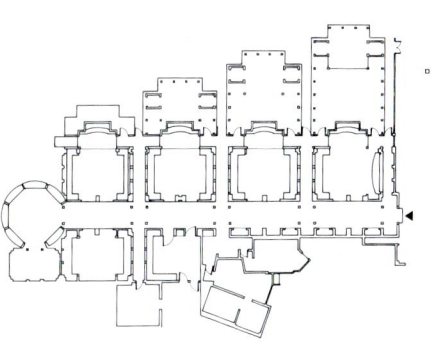

②

③

CORINTIA ⟨San Francisco⟩

Situated in "Ramada Renaissance Hotel," "CORINTIA" serves north Italian cuisines in new styles by utilizing fresh materials available in California, etc. Surrounded with blue velveted walls into which framed mirrors and etched glass panels are set, the interior gives an image of deep sea. Flowers arranged in a large vase in the center, crystal glassware, decorated plates, pin-spotted shining silver knives and forks — all these are helping create an elegant and sophisticated atmosphere in the restaurant.

● CORINTIA (San Francisco)
Address/Ramada Renaissance Hotel, 55 City Magnin Street San Francisco, CA. 94102·2865
Phone/415-392-8000
Opened/October 1984; Number of seats/60;
Number of employees/12

「ラマダ ルネッサンス ホテル」のなかにある「コリンティア」は カリフォルニア産をはじめとしたフレッシュな食材を活かした 新しいスタイルの北イタリア料理を提供している。店内は深海のイメージで ブルーのベルベット地の壁面に囲まれ その中にフレームの付いたミラーやエッチドグラスのパネルがはめ込まれている。そして中央の大きな花瓶に飾られた生花 クリスタルのグラス類 飾り皿 ピンスポットに輝くシルバーのナイフやフォークなどの小道具類が このレストラン空間のエレガンスさと高級感を演出している。

●コリンティア ⟨サンフランシスコ⟩
Address/Ramada Renaissance Hotel,55 City Magnin Street San Francisco, CA.94102·2865
Phone/415-392-8000 開店/1984年10月 客席数/60席 従業員数/12人

①

(Photo captions)
1 / The dining area gives us an image of deep sea with an elegant, formal, and sophisticated atmosphere.
2 / The wine cellar.
3 / The large etched glass placed by the table seating area in the center.

1/深海を思わせるダイニング フォーマルな高級感を演出している
2/ワインセラー
3/中央のテーブル席に置かれた大きなエッチドグラス

②

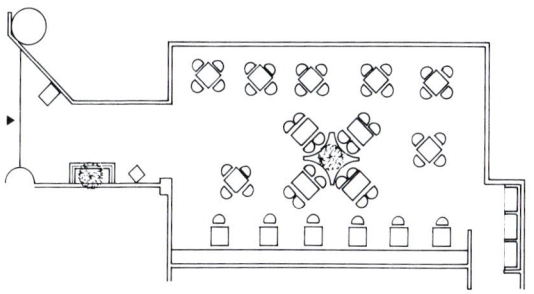

THE OLD SPAGHETTI FACTORY ⟨Hollywood, CA.⟩

A free-standing restaurant facing the Sunset Boulevard, "THE OLD SPAGHETTI FACTORY" features a flat and unique facade, and the antique interior presents gorgeousness as a dinner restaurant. Nevertheless, it serves cheap spaghetti. Headquartered in Portland, Oregon, "THE OLD SPAGHETTI FACTORY" is developing its chain. The dignified interior on the entrance area, chandeliers, mantlepiece, oval mirror, windows, lighting appliances, etc. in the grand hall — all these decor elements are genuine articles. Apart from the taste for and sense of combination of various antique pieces, such adherence to genuine articles for shop design is highly appreciated.

● THE OLD SPAGHETTI FACTORY (Hollywood)
Address/5939 Sunset Boulevard Hollywood, CA.
Number of seats/625 (restaurant 550, bar 75)

ハリウッドのサンセット大通り (Sunset Boulevard) に面して建つ フリースタンディングのフラットで ユニークな外観のこのレストランは アンティークのインテリアで豪華さを演出し 安価でスパゲティを提供するディナーレストランである。「スパゲティ ファクトリー」はオレゴン州のポートランドに本社を置きチェーン展開している。店内 入口廻りの重厚なインテリアや 大広間のシャンデリア マントルピースやオーバルのミラー 窓や照明器具などすべて本物を使用している。多くのアンティークのコレクションを取り入れ 組み合わせる好みやセンスは別にして これほどまでに本物にこだわり徹底した店づくりのユニークさが評価される。

● ジ オールド スパゲティ ファクトリー〈カリフォルニア・ハリウッド〉
Address/5939 Sunset Boulevard Hollywood, CA.
客席数/625席 (レストラン550席 バー75席)

(Photo captions)
1 / The facade imaging the Parthenon, Greece.
2 / The waiting room; all articles are composed of vintage antique pieces.
3 / The dining room; antique lighting appliances and pieces of furniture differ in shape and age, but as a whole, they create a gorgeous and composed atmosphere.

1/ギリシャのパルテノンをイメージしたファサード
2/ウェイティングルーム すべて年代物のアンティークで構成している
3/ダイニングルーム アンティークの照明器具やファニチュアは同じ形 年代のものはないが 豪華で落ち着きのある雰囲気を醸しだしている

フランス料理レストラン

ロタンダ レストラン〈サンフランシスコ〉 96
マックスウエルス プラム〈サンフランシスコ〉 98
ラ シャミエール〈ロサンゼルス〉 100
ラスコー〈サンフランシスコ〉 102
ジルス レストラン〈サンフランシスコ〉 104
ザ スカイルーム〈カリフォルニア・ロングビーチ〉 106
アンリ〈ニューオーリンズ〉 108
ザ トエンティワン クラブ〈ニューヨーク〉 110
マ メゾン〈ロサンゼルス〉 112
オランジェリー〈ロサンゼルス〉 114
ザ コロネイド レストラン〈ワシントンD.C.〉 116
フルヌーズ オープン〈サンフランシスコ〉 118
カメリオンズ〈サンタモニカ〉 120
シャンパーニュ〈ロサンゼルス〉 122
カフェ 21〈シカゴ〉 124
シトラス〈ロサンゼルス〉 126

French restaurants

ROTUNDA RESTAUTRANT ⟨San Francisco⟩ 96

MAXWELL'S PLUM ⟨San Francisco⟩ 98

LA CHAUMIERE ⟨Los Angeles⟩ 100

LASCAUX ⟨San Francisco⟩ 102

JIL'S RESTAURANT ⟨San Francisco⟩ 104

THE SKYROOM ⟨Long Beach, CA.⟩ 106

HENRI ⟨New Orleans⟩ 108

THE 21 CLUB ⟨New York⟩ 110

MA MAISON ⟨Los Angeles⟩ 112

L'ORANGERIE ⟨Los Angeles⟩ 114

THE COLONNADE RESTAURANT ⟨Washington D.C.⟩ 116

FOURNOU'S OVEN ⟨San Francisco⟩ 118

CAMELIONS ⟨Santa Monica⟩ 120

CHAMPAGNE ⟨Los Angeles⟩ 122

CAFE 21 ⟨Chicago⟩ 124

CITRUS ⟨Los Angeles⟩ 126

ROTUNDA RESTAURANT ⟨San Francisco⟩

A restaurant situated on the 4th floor of department store "Nieman Marcus" which stands on a corner of Union Square, San Francisco. The 4-storied building has a stairwell and the domed ceiling is composed of 26,000 pieces of stained glass. Constructed in 1909, the dome was moved to the present location. The name "ROTUNDA" means a "round building with a round roof." The main booth seating area is secured by a balcony along hand-carved handrails under the oval dome. The inside space is also composed of three small rooms, a bar, a waiting area, etc. which are uniformly toned in gold, white and ivory. Tableware has been strictly selected.

● ROTUNDA RESTAURANT
(San Francisco)
Address/150 Stockton San Francisco, CA. 94108
Opened/November 1982; Number of seats/178

サンフランシスコのユニオン スクエアの一角 百貨店「ニーマン マーカス(Neiman Marcus)」の4階にある。地上4階建のこの建物は吹抜けになっており 天井部は26,000ピースのステンドグラスで構成されたドームになっている。これは1909年に造られたものを移築したもので 店名の「ロタンダ」とは"丸屋根のある円形建物"の意味である。メインのブース席が 楕円形のドームの下にある手彫りの手摺りにそったバルコニーのそばに展開し 他に3つの小部屋とバー ウェイティングエリアなどで構成され ゴールドとホワイト アイボリーの色調に統一されている。食器類は特に厳選されたものを使用している。

● ロタンダ レストラン〈サンフランシスコ〉
Address/150 Stockton San Francisco, CA.94108
開店/1982年11月　客席数/178席

(Photo captions)
1・2 / The restaurant on the 4th floor of the stained glassed domed building; natural light streams into the interior, creating a gorgeous atmosphere.
3 / The dining area.

1・2/ステンドグラスのドームの4階にあるレストラン
　　店内は自然光を受け豪華な雰囲気
3/ダイニング

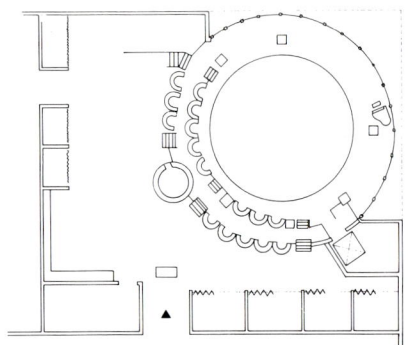

MAXWELL'S PLUM ⟨San Francisco⟩

Situated in the Ghirardelli Square, San Francisco, "MAXWELL'S PLUM" stands facing the San Francisco Bay. Designed by Mr. Warner Leroy, who is also a stage decorator, the interior is composed of four dining rooms ("Bay Room," "Crystal Room," "Fountain Room & Cafe," etc.), a bar area, and three banquet rooms. Crystal and brass chandeliers are suspended from the ceiling which is decorated with stained glasses, bronze, plaster, etc., while 50 pieces of art nouveau and art deco statues are decorated. The restaurant is closed now.

● MAXWELL'S PLUM (San Francisco)
Closed now; Opened/May 1981; Number of seats/512 (bay room 191, crystal room 100, fountain room & cafe 121, bar 100), Banquet room (maximum capacity 20); Number of employees/280

サンフランシスコのギャラリー スクエアー内のサンフランシスコ湾に面して建つ「マックスウエルス プラム」。デザインは舞台装飾家でもあるワーナー リロイ(Warner Leroy)氏で"ベイ ルーム""クリスタル ルーム""ファウンテン ルーム&カフェ"などの4つのダイニング バーエリア 3室のバンケットルームで構成されている。店内にはクリスタルやブラスのシャンデリアが ステンドグラスやブロンズ 石膏などで装飾された天井から吊り下げられ 50点のアールヌーボーやアールデコの彫刻が飾られている。このレストランは現在閉店されている。

●マックスウエルス プラム〈サンフランシスコ〉
現在閉店中 開店/1981年5月 客席数/512席(ベイ ルーム191席 クリスタル ルーム100席 ファウンテン ルーム&カフェ121席 バー100席) バンケット ルーム(最大320人収容) 従業員数/280人

(Photo captions)
1/ "Crystal Room"; the chandeliers and crystal on the wall present gorgeousness.
2/ The bar area; light from the chandeliers is reflected in the bronze relief on the ceiling, creating a unique atmosphere.
3/ "Bay Room" which features wonderful stained glasses on the ceiling; the guest seating area is surrounded with fresh flowers.

1/"クリスタル ルーム" シャンデリアや壁画のクリスタルが豪華さを演出
2/バーエリア シャンデリアの光が天井のブロンズのレリーフに反射 独特の雰囲気を醸し出している
3/天井のステンドグラスがみごとな"ベイ ルーム"客席は新鮮な花で囲まれている

LA CHAUMIERE ⟨Los Angeles⟩

The name "LA CHAUMIERE" means, in French, a "quiet rest house in a French countryside." It is a formal restaurant of the "Century Plaza Hotel Tower" (322 rooms on 30 floors). The interior is composed of a main dining area in the dignified European club style and "Winter Garden" which has a soft atmosphere like a terrace, in sharp contrast to the main dining area, and decorated with the 18th to 19th century French landscape paintings, a large antique clock, etc. Born in Germany, the chef Raimund Hofmeister offers a menu of unique cuisine.
● LA CHAUMIERE (Los Angeles)
Address/Century Plaza Hotel, 2025 Avenue of The Stars Century City Los Angeles, CA. 90067
Pnone/213-277-2000

Opened/December 1984; Number of seats/ 114

(Photo captions)
1 / The reception; decorated with the large antique clock and a collection of landscape paintings drawn in the latter half of the 19th century.
2 / The main dining area; in the dignified European club style.
3 / The terrace-like "Winter Garden" has an atmosphere which sharply contrasts with that of the main dining area.

1/レセプション　アンティークの大時計や19世紀後半に描かれた風景画などのコレクションが飾られている
2/メインダイニング　格調高いヨーロッパのクラブ風の造り
3/テラス風の"ウィンター ガーデン"メインダイニングとは対象的な雰囲気

店名はフランス語で"田舎の静養所"の意味。「センチュリー プラザ ホテル タワー」(地上30階建 322室)のフォーマルレストランである。インテリアは格調高いヨーロッパのクラブ風の造りのメインダイニングと 対象的にテラス風のソフトな雰囲気の"ウインターガーデン"で構成。店内には 18〜19世紀のフランスの風景画やアンティークの大時計などのコレクションが並べられている。シェフはドイツ生まれのRaimund Hofmeister氏で独特のメニューを生み出し提供している。
● ラ シャミエール⟨ロサンゼルス⟩
Address/Century Plaza Hotel, 2025 Avenue of The Stars Century City Los Angeles, CA. 90067　Phone/213-277-2000　開店/1984年12月　客席数/114席

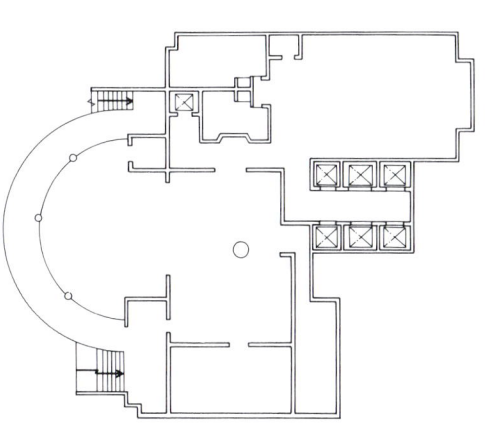

②

③

LASCAUX 〈San Francisco〉

"LASCAUX" is composed of a gallery on the 1st floor and a restaurant in the basement. The basement is likened to an underground treasure house where pieces of ancient art are concealed. It serves European homemade meals cooked by the owner-chef Annette Esser. Designed by Mr. Pat Kuleto, the interior is decorated with paintings and sculpture, forming a composed presentation. A rich collection of wine is displayed in the wine cellar.

● LASCAUX (San Francisco)
Address/248 Sutter Street San Francisco, CA.
Phone/415-391-1555
Opened/October 1988;　Number of seats/210 (dining room 150, bar 60);　Number of employees/60

(Photo captions)
1 / The dining area imaging an art museum.
2 / The dining area with a fireplace; unique presentation of napkins.
3 / The facade; a gallery on the 1st floor and a restaurant in the basement.

1/美術館をイメージしたダイニングエリア
2/暖炉があるダイニング　ナプキンの演出がユニーク
3/ファサード　1階はギャラリーで地階がレストランになっている

「ラスコー」は　1階のギャラリーと地階のレストランで構成されている。古代美術が眠る地下の宝庫をレストランにしたという設定。料理はこの店のオーナー　シェフ Annette Esser さんがヨーロッパの家庭料理を提供している。インテリアは　Pat Kuleto 氏で美術館をイメージした店内には絵画や彫刻が飾られ　落ち着いた空間演出になっている。また豊富なワインのコレクションが　ダイニングに併設されたワインセラーにならべられている。

●ラスコー〈サンフランシスコ〉
Address/248 Sutter Street San Francisco, CA.
Phone/415-391-1555　開店/1988年10月　客席数/210席(ダイニングルーム150席　バー60席)　従業員数/60人

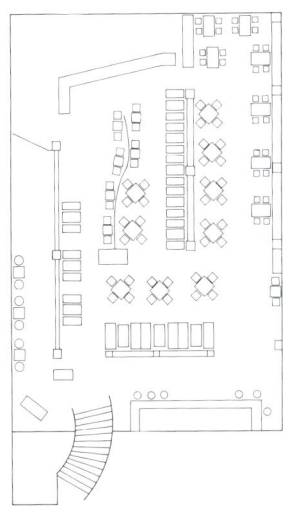

JIL'S RESTAURANT ⟨San Francisco⟩

A restaurant jointly managed by three young Dutch owners who graduated from a professional school on hotels & restaurants in Hague, and the menu is composed of unique mixtures of European and American foods. The interior is decorated with pieces of art by young European artists, thus creating a new-type bistro by combining the European and American senses. This restaurant is closed now.
● JIL'S RESTAURANT (San Francisco)
Closed now; Opened/February 1987, Number of seats/160 (restaurant 130, bar 30); Number of employees/20

(Photo captions)
1 / The new bistro-style dining room introducing the European & American senses.
2 / The wall side table seating corner with sofa is favorably accepted by young couples.
3 / The dining room; the wall is decorated with pieces of art by young European artists.
4 / The bar counter; glass sales of wine are also active.
5 / The facade of the restaurant which stands near the Union Square.

1/ユーロピアン＆アメリカンの感覚を取り入れた 新しいビストロスタイルのダイニング ルーム
2/壁側のソファのあるテーブル席はカップル客に人気
3/ダイニングの壁面には ヨーロッパの若いアーティストたちの作品が飾られている
4/バーカウンター ワインのショット売りもしている
5/ファサード レストランはユニオンスクエアから近い

ハーグのホテル レストランの専門学校出身の若い3人のオランダ人が共同経営する店で ヨーロッパとアメリカ料理をミックスさせた新しいメニューを提供している。店内にはヨーロッパ出身の若いアーティストたちの作品が飾られヨーロッパとアメリカの感覚を合わせ持つ 新しいビストロスタイルを造りだしている。このレストランは現在閉店されている。
●ジルス レストラン⟨サンフランシスコ⟩
現在閉店中 開店/1987年2月 客席数/160席（レストラン130席 バー30席） 従業員数/20人

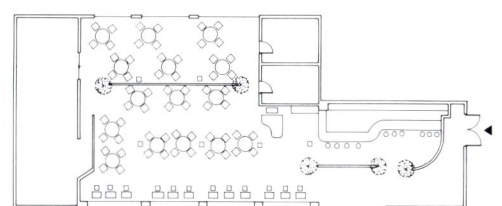

THE SKYROOM 〈Long Beach, CA.〉

A French restaurant on the highest floor of 14-storied "The Breakers Hotel" which stands along Long Beach. Designed by Mr. Scheer Braden, the interior employs Hawaiian motif and art deco elements. He installed neon tubes on the ceiling, columns, glass block walls, etc., thus producing colored lighting effects in the white & blue dining space which has open windows.

● THE SKYROOM (Long Beach, CA.)
Address/The Breakers Hotel, 210 East Ocean Boulevard Long Beach, CA. 90802
Phone/213-432-8781
Opened/February 1984

(Photo captions)
1 / The dining room employing Hawaiian motif and art deco design.
2 / The bar counter.
3 / The entrance; with the tropically lighted wine cellar.
4 / The wine cellar and lobby viewed from the bar lounge.

1/ハワイ風のモチーフとアールデコのデザインを取り入れたダイニングルーム
2/バーカウンター
3/エントランス トロピカルな照明のワインセラーがある
4/バーラウンジよりワインセラーとロビーをみる

ロングビーチの海岸に沿って建つ14階建の「ザ ブリーカーズホテル」の最上階にあるフランス料理レストランで ハワイ風のモチーフとアールデコのデザインを取り入れている。デザインはScheer Braden氏で ネオン管を天井や円柱 ガラスブロックの壁面などに配し 開放的な窓を持つ白とブルーのダイニングのなかで 色による照明効果をあげている。

● ザ スカイルーム〈カリフォルニア・ロングビーチ〉
Address/The Breakers Hotel, 210 East Ocean Boulevard Long Beach, CA.90802 Phone/213-432-8781 開店/1984年2月

②

③

④

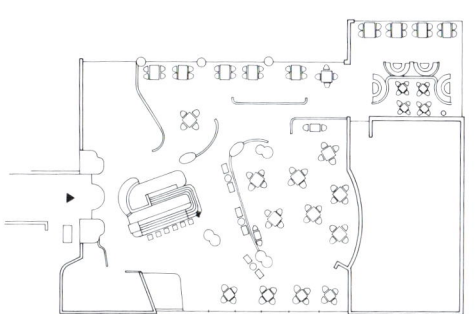

HENRI ⟨New Orleans⟩

"HENRI" is a French restaurant operating in the "Meridien Hotel." As consultant and chef patron, Mr. Marc Haeberlin was invited from "Auberge de l'Ill," a three-star restaurant in Alsace, France. Excellent service by a good combination with the chef Patrick Granito and maître Yves Jouanno is favorably accepted by guests. The neo-classic interior is chicly designed with green-toned paintings of European châteaus, royalty and nobility, and gorgeous chandeliers in the bar, marbled service station, etc.

● HENRI (New Orleans)
Address/Hotel Meridien New Orleans, 614 Canal Street New Orleans, Louisiana 70130
Phone/504-527-7808
Opened/December 1984; Number of seats/120 (1st floor 70, 2nd floor 50); Number of employees/16

「アンリ」は「メリディアンホテル」内にあるフランス料理レストラン。フランスのアルザスの三つ星レストラン「オーベルジュ ドゥ リル (Auberge de l'Ill)」のマルク エーベルラン (Marc Haeberlin)氏をコンサルタントとシェフパトロンとして迎え シェフのPatrick Granito氏と メートルのYves Jouanno氏の息の合ったサービスが好評。ネオクラシック調の店内はグリーンを基調にしたヨーロッパのシャトーや王侯貴族を描いた絵画や豪華なシャンデリア大理石のバーやサービスステーションなどでシックにまとめられている。

●アンリ〈ニューオリンズ〉
Address/Hotel Meridien New Orleans, 614 Canal Street New Orleans, Louisiana 70130
Phone/504-527-7808　開店/1984年12月　客席数/120席(1階70席　2階50席)　従業員数/16人

(Photo captions)
1 / The interior is in neo-classic style decorated with paintings of European châteaus, royalty and nobility.
2 / Gorgeousness presented with chandeliers, marbled service station, etc.
3 / The marbled bar counter.
4 / The entrance.

1/ヨーロッパのシャトーや王侯貴族を描いた絵画があるネオクラシック調の店内
2/シャンデリアや大理石のサービスステーションなど豪華さを演出している
3/大理石のバーカウンター
4/エントランス

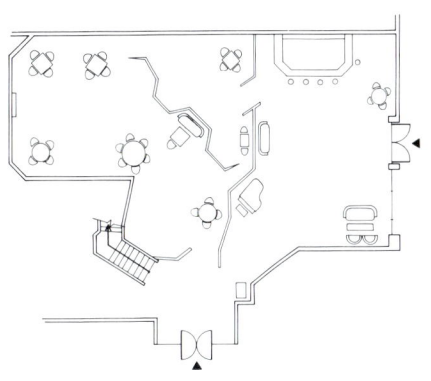

THE 21 CLUB 〈New York〉

The facade of "THE 21 CLUB," a dinner restaurant in Manhattan, is known for lined display of jockey champion dolls. The restaurant is composed of a bar corner, dining area and waiting room on the 1st floor, and a main dining area on the 2nd floor. From the ceiling of the 1st floor, derby hats, miniature automobiles, ships and airplanes are suspended, while the walls are decorated with a collection related to horce racing, beer jugs, etc., thus creating a casual, amusing atmosphere. On the other hand, the main dining area on the 2nd floor has a composed atmosphere under nearly indirect lighting, giving a traditional impression with polished silver plates differing in size which decorate the wall.
● THE 21 CLUB (New York)
Address/21 West 52nd Street New York, N.Y.

マンハッタンのディナーレストラン「ザ トエンティワン クラブ」のファサードは 競馬の優勝騎手の人形をずらりと並べたユニークさで知られている。レストランは1階のバーコーナーとダイニング ウエィティングルームと2階のメインダイニングで構成されている。1階は天井からジョッキーの帽子やミニチュアの自動車 船 飛行機がぶらさげられ 壁面には競馬に関するコレクションやビールのジョッキがかざられカジュアルで楽しい雰囲気でまとめられている。2階のメインダイニングは 間接に近い照明が落ち着いた雰囲気を盛り上げ 壁面には磨き上げられた大小のシルバーの盛り皿が飾られ伝統あるレストランの威厳を感じさせる。
●ザ トエンティワン クラブ 〈ニューヨーク〉
Address/21 West 52nd Street New York, N.Y.

(Photo captions)
1 / The unique facade with lined dolls of jockey champions which welcome guests.
2 / The 2nd floor main dining area having a dignified atmosphere characteristic of a traditional high-class restaurant.
3・4 / The 1st floor dining & bar featuring derby hats, miniature automobiles, airplanes, etc.

1/競馬の優勝ジョッキーの人形がずらりと並んで客を迎えるユニークなファサード
2/伝統的な高級レストランの威厳を持つ2階のメインダイニング
3・4/ミニチュアの自動車や飛行機 ジョッキーの帽子などがぶらさげられた1階のダイニング&バー

②

MA MAISON ⟨Los Angeles⟩

Standing on the opposite side of the high-class shopping center "Beverly Center," and adjacent to the hotel "Sofitel," "MA MAISON" serves new-type French cuisine. The owner is Mr. Patrick A. Terrail, nephew of the owner of "Tour d'Argnt" in Paris. The glassed interior space is designed to introduce natural light by installing a sky light in the center of the main dining space. By employing a variety of trees and greenery, the interior is presented to look like an elegant patio.
● MA MAISON (Los Angeles)
Address/8555 Beverly Boulevard Los Angeles, CA. 90048
Phone/213-655-1991
Opened/December 1988;　Number of seats/154 (dining 138, bar 16)

高級ショッピングセンター「ビバリー センター(Beverly Center)」の向い側　ホテル「Sofitel」に隣接する　新しいスタイルのフランス料理を提供するレストラン。オーナーはパリの「トゥール ダルジャン(Tour d'Argnt)」の主人の甥にあたるPatrick A. Terrail氏。ガラス張りの店内はメインダイニングの中央部に天窓を設け　自然光を取り入れている。多くの樹木やグリーンを持ち込み　エレガントなパティオ風に演出している。
●マ メゾン〈ロサンゼルス〉
Address/8555 Beverly Boulevard Los Angeles, CA.90048　Phone/213-655-1991　開店/1988年12月　客席数/154席(ダイニング138席　バー16席)

(Photo captions)
1 / The main dining area; designed to introduce natural light from the sky light so that it looks like a patio.
2 / The bar area has a homely atmosphere.
3 / The bright glassed appearance.
4 / The main dining area at dinnertime whose atmosphere becomes even more elegant at night.

1/メインダイニング　天窓から自然光を取り入れたパティオ風な演出
2/バーエリアはアットホームな雰囲気
3/ガラス張りの明るい外観
4/昼と夜ではすっかり趣きが異なり　よりエレガントな雰囲気のメインダイニング

L'ORANGERIE ⟨Los Angeles⟩

Featuring a château-like facade which faces La Cienega Boulevard, "L'ORANGERIE" is a French restaurant owned by Mr. Gerard Ferry and his wife Vivginie Ferry who are French. From foods to interior and service, the restaurant clings to the "images of France," and employed the architectural style in the 17th century which became fashionable from the days of Louis 14th; the trees are installed so that they harmonize with the interior. Arched surrounds above the windows and doors are provided to grow orange trees indoors. A patio seating space is secured in the center, and the areas near the arched windows and doors are rich with trees and green plants.

● L'ORANGERIE (Los Angeles)
Address/903 North La Cienega Boulevard Los Angeles, CA.
Opened/1978

(Photo captions)
1 / The patio seating area; uniformly toned in blue, in contrast to the colorful dining room.
2・4 / The colorful dining room employing the European architectural style in the 17th century.
3 / Facing La Cienega Boulevard, the facade looks like a château.

1／パティオ席　カラフルなダイニングルームとは対象的にブルー系で統一している
2・4／17世紀のヨーロッパの建築様式を取り入れたカラフルなダイニングルーム
3／ラ シェネガ通りに面したシャトー風の外観

ラ シェネガ通り（La Cienega Boulevard）に面して建つ　シャトー風の外観を持つ「オランジェリー」は　フランス人のジェラルド フェリィ（Gerard and Vivginie Ferry）夫妻がオーナーのフレンチレストランである。料理やインテリア サービスに至るまで"フランスのイメージ"にこだわりを持ち　建物にはルイ14世以後に流行した　17世紀の建築様式を取り入れ　樹木がインテリアにマッチするようにデザインしたという。高いアーチを持たせた窓やドアは冬の間室内でオレンジの木を育てるためのもの。レストランの中央部にパティオ席を配し　アーチの窓やドアのあたりには樹木などグリーンのプラントをふんだんに取り入れている。

●オランジェリー〈ロサンゼルス〉
Address/903 North La Cienega Boulevard Los Angelse, CA.　開店／1978年

②

③

④

THE COLONNADE RESTAURANT ⟨Washington D.C.⟩

This restaurant serves as the main dining space of "Westin Hotel." Detached from the hotel building, it stands like a French château in the 18th century, facing the hotel's courtyard. In addition to the large French style windows, elegant crystal chandeliers and glazed dome, the dining space also features the brightly carpeted floor, accented with pieces of French crystal glassware on the white table cloth.

● THE COLONNADE RESTAURANT (Washington D.C.)
Address/2401 M. Street N. W. Washington D.C. 20037
Phone/202-429-2400
Opened/December 1985, Number of seats/140; Number of employees/35

このレストランは 「ウェスティン ホテル (Westin Hotel)」のメインダイニングで ホテル棟とは別に 中庭に面した18世紀のフランスのシャトー風の外観の建物である。大きなフランス式の窓 エレガントなクリスタルのシャンデリア 中央にグラスドームの天井を設けたダイニングのフロアには明るいデザインのじゅうたんが敷かれ 白いテーブルクロスの上のフレンチクリスタルのグラス類がアクセントとなっている。

● ザ コロネイド レストラン⟨ワシントン D.C.⟩
Address/2401 M.Street N.W.Washington D.C. 20037 Phone/202-429-2400 開店/1985年12月 客席数/140席 従業員数/35人

(Photo captions)
1・2 / The facade looks like a French Château; with the copper plate roofing with a dome.
3 / The dining space with a glazed dome in the center.
4 / The interior viewed from the reception area; the floor is covered with a bright carpet.

1・2/フランスのシャトー風の外観 銅板の屋根にドームを配している
3/中央部にグラスドームを設けたダイニング
4/レセプションから店内をみる フロアには明るいデザインのじゅうたんが敷かれている

②

FOURNOU'S OVEN ⟨San Francisco⟩

This forms an extension to the existing restaurant of "Stanford Court Hotel" in San Francisco. Facing California Street, "FOURNOU'S OVEN" has been designed so that guests can enjoy viewing outside scenery, while making the facade appeal to riders on cable cars which go up and down the slope. The exterior looks like an old European hothouse whose roof line is curved, thus harmonizing well with the surrounding scenery. The interior is composed of an extension which looks like a bright garden terrace and the existing Spanish dining area which has a composed atmosphere. An old oven after which the restaurant was named, is preserved in the inner dining space.
● FOURNOU'S OVEN (San Francisco)
Address/Nob Hill San Francisco, CA. 94108
Opened/April 1979;   Number of seats/300
(dining 175, bar 125)

サンフランシスコの「スタンフォード コート ホテル」のレストランで 既存のレストランに増設したもの。カリフォルニア ストリートに面して建つこのレストランは 内部からの眺望と坂道を上下するケーブルカーの乗客の視線に訴えるデザインでまとめたという。外観は上部が曲線を描いたヨーロッパの古い温室風で 周辺の景観にも調和している。店内は明るいガーデンテラス風の増設部分と 既存の落ち着いたスペイン調のダイニングで構成されている。店名の由来の古いオーブンが既存のダイニングの奥に残されている。
●フルヌーズ オーブン ⟨サンフランシスコ⟩
Address/Nob Hill San Francisco, CA.94108 開店/1979年4月 客席数/300席(ダイニング175席 バー125席)

(Photo captions)
1・2 / The dining area — an extension — looks like a bright terrace.
3 / The arched aisle leading to the existing dining space.
4 / The old oven after which the restaurant was named.

1・2/増設された 明るいガーデンテラス風のダイニング
3/既存のダイニングへのアーチのある通路
4/店名の由来となった 古いオーブン

②

③

④

119

CAMELIONS ⟨Santa Monica⟩

"Camelion" is a medieval English word corresponding to the present "chameleon" and has been adopted by the owner Marsha Sans to imply that the restaurant responds adequately from time to time by changing the menu. The restaurant serves French cuisine cooked by utilizing California materials. Located on a high-class residential quarter in Santa Monica, "CAMELIONS" has been designed by Mr. John Buyers who redecorated an old Spanish residence.

● CAMELIONS (Santa Monica)
Address/246 26th Street Santa Monica, CA. 9002
Phone/213-395-0746
Number of seats/149 (main dining 49, terrace, private room 100); Number of employees/40

店名は中世の英語で 現在のカメレオン(chameleon)と同意語 その時々に応じメニューを変え 適切な対応をするレストランという意味を含めて女性オーナーのマーシャ サンズ(Marsha Sans)さんが名づけたという。メニューはカリフォルニア産の素材を活かしたフランス料理。サンタモニカの高級住宅地に立地し デザインはジョン バイヤーズ(John Buyers)氏で 古いスペイン調の住宅を改装したもの。

●カメレオンズ⟨サンタモニカ⟩
Address/246 26th Street Santa Monica, CA. 9002 Phone/213-395-0746 客席数/149席(メインダイニング49席 テラス席 プライベートルーム100席) 従業員数/40人

①

②

(Photo captions)
1 / The patio and dining room are also opened as a reception.
2 / The open-air terrace seating space; popular at lunch time.
3 / The Spanish dining room accented with a fireplace.

1/パティオとダイニングルームはレセプションにも開放している
2/オープンエアのテラス席 ランチタイムには人気
3/暖炉があるスペイン風のダイニング

CHAMPAGNE ⟨Los Angeles⟩

A French-Californian restaurant whose facade puts up a logo mark of champagne bubbles. The menu is composed of a variety of new-type cuisine cooked by the young owner-chef Patrick Healy. The simply designed interior is brightly decorated with fresh flowers and accented with contemporary paintings on the walls. Situated in a residential quarter on the western side of Century City, the restaurant has succeeded in covering the conditions of location which are not necessarily favorable, by serving new-type cuisine and employing simple interior, table setting, etc.
● CHAMPAGNE (Los Angeles)
Address/10506 Santa Monica Boulevard Los Angeles, CA. 90025
Phone/213-470-8446
Opened/October 1987;   Number of seats/100;   Number of employees/30

シャンペンの泡が立ち上るロゴマークのフレンチ カリフォルニア料理店。若いオーナーシェフのPatrick Healyが 調理する新しいバラエティに富むメニューを用意しているのが特徴。明るくシンプルなデザインの店内にはフレッシュな花が飾られ 壁面に掛けられたコンテンポラリーな絵画がアクセントになっている。センチュリーシティの西側の住宅地に位置するこのレストランは 新しい料理とサービス シンプルさを強調したインテリアやテーブルセッティングなどで 決して良いとはいえないロケーションの条件をカバーし成功している。
●シャンパーニュ〈ロサンゼルス〉
Address/10506 Santa Monica Boulevard Los Angeles, CA.90025   Phone/213-470-8446   開店/1987年10月   客席数/100席   従業員数/30名

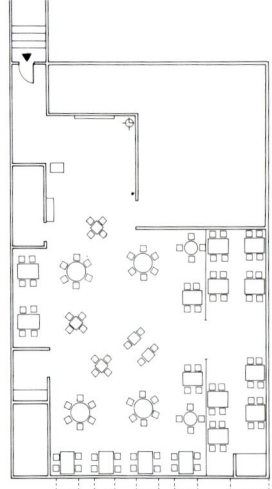

(Photo captions)
1 / Accented with paintings on the wall.
2 / The facade facing Santa Monica Boulevard; accented with the yellow sunshade tent and white signboard which stand out against the blue sky.
3 / The simple and bright dining area; decorated with fresh flowers.

1/壁面に掛けられた絵画がアクセントになっている
2/サンタモニカ通りに面したファサード 黄色い日除けのテントと白いサインボードが青空に映える
3/シンプルで明るいダイニングエリア フレッシュな花が飾られている

CAFE 21 〈Chicago〉

"CAFE 21" is the main dining room on the 2nd floor of "Hotel 21 East." The chef Martin Gagne offers a new menu of "contemporary American cuisine" by intersecting French, Italian and southwestern American ingredients. Facing the street, the dining space is designed in the post-modern style by securing two large glazed window sides. The wall is decorated with flower photos taken by photographer Robert Mappelethorpe. The restaurant is closed now.

● CAFE 21 (Chicago)
Closed now;   Opened/1988;   Number of seats/74

(Photo captions)
1・3 / The horseshoe-shaped bar counter area; composed of the copper counter, leathered chairs and marble floor.
2 / The post-modern dining room; the wall is decorated with flower photos.

シカゴの「Hotel 21 East」の2階にある 同ホテルのメインダイニングルームである。シェフのMartin Gagne は コンテンポラリー アメリカン キュイジーンとして フランス イタリア 及びアメリカ西南部の料理を交差させた新しいメニューづくりをし提供している。通りに面し2方をガラスで包む大きな窓を設けたダイニングはポストモダンの造り。壁面には 写真家Robert Mappelethorpeが撮影した花の写真が飾られている。このレストランは現在閉店している。

●カフェ 21 〈シカゴ〉
現在閉店中　開店/1988年　客席数/74席

1・3/馬蹄形のバーカウンター 銅製のカウンター レザーのチェア 大理石のフロアで構成されている
2/ポストモダンのダイニング 壁面には花の写真が飾られている

①

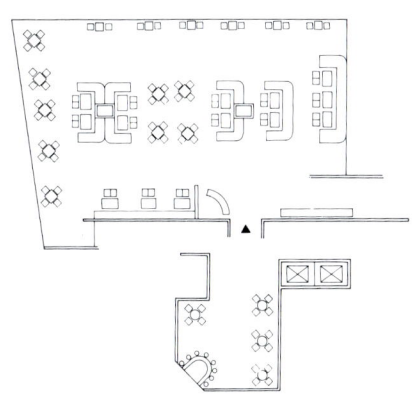

CITRUS 〈Los Angeles〉

The name "CITRUS" means "citrus fruits." Using white as the basic tone, the interior is arranged in a bright Californian space and employs modern artistic elements. The owner-chef Michel Richard does not use butter or cream, but heavily uses purée of vegetables base on consommé or olive oil. These health and calorie oriented foods with taste and color are very popular.
● CITRUS (Los Angeles)
Address/6703 Melrose Avenue Los Angeles, CA. 90038
Phone/213-857-0034
Opened/February 1987;   Number of seats/190;   Number of employees/85

店名は"柑橘類"という意味。店内はホワイトを基調にし カリフォルニアらしい明るい空間に モダンでアーティスティックなインテリアで構成している。オーナー シェフのミシェル リチャード(Michel Richard)氏の調理法は バターやクリームを使用せず ソースはコンソメをベースに 野菜類のピューレやオリーブオイルを多用するのが特徴で ヘルシーやカロリー指向に味と色彩を加えた料理が好評。
●シトラス〈ロサンゼルス〉
Address/6703 Melrose Avenue Los Angeles, CA.90038 Phone/213-857-0034 開店/1987年2月 客席数/190席 従業員数/85人

(Photo captions)
1 / The modern, white facade facing Melrose Avenue.
2 / The impressive objet by a modern artist stands by the entrance.
3 / The dining area looks like a terrace with parasols.
4 / The entrance hall having a formal atmosphere spreads towards your across the bar area (right side); behind them the terrace-like dining area is visible.

1/メルロース通りに面した白いモダンなファサード
2/モダンアーティストのオブジェが入口に立ち印象づける
3/店内にパラソルを立てテラス風に演出されたダイニング
4/エントランスホール バーエリア(右)をはさんで 手前に広がるフォーマルな感じのダイニング 後方にテラス風ダイニング

②

①

③

④

カジュアル & ディナーレストラン-1

ロザリーズ〈サンフランシスコ〉 130
ディーシー スリー〈サンタモニカ〉 132
メサ グリル〈ニューヨーク〉 134
アメリーク〈シカゴ〉 136
スピード 690〈サンフランシスコ〉 138
パイプライン〈ニューヨーク〉 140
ビスタンゴ〈カリフォルニア・アーバイン〉 142
ステラス プレイス〈シカゴ〉 144
スパゴ カリフォルニア キュイジーヌ〈ロサンゼルス〉 146
ロビンス〈ニューヨーク〉 148
タンブルウィード〈カリフォルニア・ビバリーヒルズ〉 150
ハード ロック カフェ〈ロサンゼルス〉 152
レストラン&バー アット モーガンズ〈ニューヨーク〉 153
サターニア〈ニューヨーク〉 154
ジム マクマホンズ〈シカゴ〉 156
ポストリオ レストラン〈サンフランシスコ〉 158
アウト テイクス〈シカゴ〉 160
ゴードン〈シカゴ〉 162
セント ジェイムス クラブ〈ロサンゼルス〉 164
シティ グリル〈ロサンゼルス〉 166
マスタング グリル〈ニューヨーク〉 168
555 イースト〈カリフォルニア・ロングビーチ〉 170

Casual & Dinner restaurants-1

ROSALIE'S ⟨San Francisco⟩ 130

DC 3 ⟨Santa Monica⟩ 132

MESA GRILL ⟨New York⟩ 134

AMÉRIQUE ⟨Chicago⟩ 136

690 SPEEDO ⟨San Francisco⟩ 138

PIPELINE ⟨New York⟩ 140

BISTANGO ⟨Irvine, CA.⟩ 142

STELLA'S PLACE ⟨Chicago⟩ 144

SPAGO CALIFORNIA CUISINE ⟨Los Angeles⟩ 146

ROBBIN'S ⟨New York⟩ 148

TUMBLEWEED ⟨Beverly Hills, CA.⟩ 150

HARD ROCK CAFE ⟨Los Angeles⟩ 152

Restaurant & Bar at MORGANS ⟨New York⟩ 153

SATURNIA ⟨New York⟩ 154

JIM MACMAHON'S ⟨Chicago⟩ 156

POSTRIO RESTAURANT ⟨San Francisco⟩ 158

OUT TAKES ⟨Chicago⟩ 160

GORDON ⟨Chicago⟩ 162

ST. JAMES'S CLUB ⟨Los Angeles⟩ 164

CITY GRILL ⟨Los Angeles⟩ 166

MUSTANG GRILL ⟨New York⟩ 168

555 EAST ⟨Long Beach, CA.⟩ 170

ROSALIE'S ⟨San Francisco⟩

A trendy restaurant in San Francisco, "ROSALIE'S" is famous for its unique and sophisticated menu compositions, such as dishing up various types of materials and flavor over a plate. The owner is Mr. Bill Belloli who was formerly a model for a cosmetics company. The wide interior space, which has been redecorated from an automobile showroom, is composed of monotoned tin-made coconut trees, tabletop finish, etc. The interior presentation is unique with naked mannequins suspended from the upper parts of the thick pillar partitions.

● ROSALIE'S (San Francisco)
Address/1415 Van Ness Avenue San Francisco, CA. 94109
Phone/415-928-7188
Opened/May 1985;   Number of seats/180 (restaurant 170, bar 10)

(Photo captions)
1 / The monotone-finished dining area; surrounded with tin-made coconut trees.
2 / The piano lounge with lined white pillow cases. Live piano performance is also offered against the unique presentation with mannequins which are looking down from the upper parts of the partition.
3 / The bar corner with comfortable cane chairs.
4 / The entrance area; formerly, the building was an automobile showroom.

1/モノトーンで構成されたダイニングエリア　ブリキ製のヤシの木に囲まれている
2/白いピロケースが並ぶピアノラウンジ　ピアノのライブ演奏も行われ　パーティションの上からはマネキンものぞきこむユニークな演出
3/ゆったりした藤椅子があるバーコーナー
4/エントランス廻り　元は車のショールームだった

いろいろな素材やフレイバーを一つの皿に盛り合わせるなど　手の込んだメニューづくりをしている「ロザリーズ」は　サンフランシスコのトレンディレストランである。オーナーは元化粧品会社のモデル Bille Belloli氏。車のショールームを改装した広い空間の店内は　ブリキ板のヤシの木やテーブルトップが目立つモノトーンカラーで構成されている。太い柱のパーティションの上部から　裸のマネキンがぶらさがったユニークな演出をしている。

●ロザリーズ⟨サンフランシスコ⟩
Address/1451 Van Ness Avenue San Francisco, CA.94109　Phone/415-928-7188　開店/1985年5月　客席数/180席(レストラン170席　バー10席)

②

③

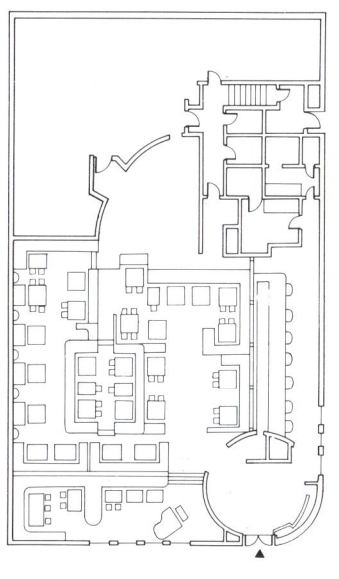
④

DC 3 ⟨Santa Monica⟩

④

⑤

⑥

Santa Monica Airport where private airplanes land and take off one after another. Jointly managed by four owners including Mr. Bruce Marder and chef Mr. William Hufferd, "DC 3" features an interior designed by imaging an airport which serves as a spacious show place.

● DC 3 (Santa Monica)
Address/2800 Donald Douglas Loop North Santa Monica, CA. 90405
Phone/213-399-2323
Opened/1988; Number of seats/392 (main dining 180, banquet room 180, private dining 32); Number of employees/130

自家用飛行機の離着陸で忙しいサンタモニカ空港。その滑走路に面して建つモダンなレストラン。Bruce Marder氏やシェフのWilliam Hufferd氏を中心にした4人のオーナーたちの共同経営による「DC 3」は 多くの現代アーティストを起用し 飛行場をテーマにしたインテリアで イメージの広い空間ショープレイスになっている。
●ディーシー スリー〈サンタモニカ〉
Address/2800 Donald Douglas Loop North SantaMonica, CA.90405   Phone/213-399-2323
開店/1988年 客席数/392席(メインダイニング180席 バンケットルーム180席 プライベートダイニング32席) 従業員数/130人

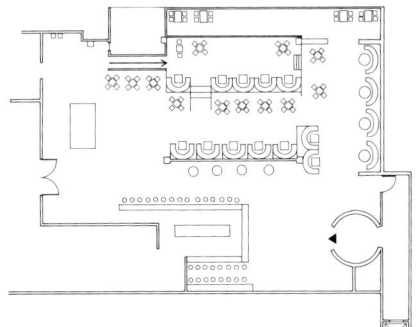

(Photo captions)
1 / The main dining room; with the round domed reception and the unique artistic title "Pacific Rim" on the wall.
2 / The main dining room featuring the reception (round dome) and the wall art.
3 / The spacious bar area with a seafood bar; the counter waist is decorated with leather.
4 / The restaurant (on the 2nd floor) adjacent to the aviation museum within the Santa Monica Airport.
5 / The see-through elevator leads to the restaurant.
6 / The reception area designed by imaging an airport checkin counter.

1/メインダイニング 円形ドームのレセプションと "パシフィック リム" と題した壁面のアートがユニーク
2/レセプション(円形ドーム)と壁面のアートがあるメインダイニング
3/シーフードバー付きの広々としたバーエリア カウンターの腰には毛皮が貼られている
4/シースルーのエレベーターがレストランに通じる
5/空港のチェックインカウンターのイメージのレセプション
6/サンタモニカ空港内の航空博物館に隣接したレストラン(2階)

MESA GRILL 〈New York〉

A restaurant in the Southwestern style situated in the Flatiron area south of Fifth Avenue where many advertising agents, publishers, artists' studios, etc. gather, "MESA GRILL" is managed by Mr. Jerry Kretchmer, owner of "Gotham Bar & Grill" and real estate developer, and Jeff Bliss. The young chef Bobby Flay, who invited by them, offers upgraded Southwestern Mexican foods accented with a more American style. The interior is drawing attention, as the designer James Biber has inspired the spirit of play into it.
● MESA GRILL (New York)
Address/102 Fifth Avenue New York, N.Y. 10011
Phone/212-807-7400
Opened/January 15, 1991; Number of seats/ 151 (dining 135, bar 16)

ニューヨークの5番街(Fifth Avenue)の南 広告代理店や出版社 芸術家たちのスタジオなどが集まるフラットアイアン地区に位置するサウス ウエスタンスタイルのレストラン。ゴッサム バー & グリル(Gotham Bar & Grill)のオーナーで不動産デベロッパーのジェリー クレッチマー(Jerry Kretchmer)氏とジェフ ブリス(Jeff Bliss)氏の経営。シェフには若いボビー フレイ(Bobby Flay)を迎え サウス ウエスタンのメキシコ調に よりアメリカンスタイルを加えアップグレードさせた料理を提供している。インテリアはジェイムス ビバー(James Biber)で遊び心をもたせ カジュアルにまとめ 話題になっている。
●メサ グリル〈ニューヨーク〉
Address/102 Fifth Avenue New York, N.Y. 10011 Phone/212-807-7400 開店1991年1月15日 客席数/151席(ダイニング135席 バー16席)

(Photo captions)
1 / The bar corner overlooked from the 2nd floor; accented with aluminum lighting equipment and wired fans which were made to special order.
2 / The table seating area; the open kitchen is visible behind.
3 / The bar corner area viewed from the inner part.

1/2階からバーコーナーを俯瞰する アルミの照明やワイヤー製のファンは特注
2/テーブル席 奥はオープンキッチン
3/店内奥よりバーコーナー方向をみる

AMÉRIQUE ⟨Chicago⟩

"AMÉRIQUE" is situated at River North which is in the north of River Chicago. This quarter has been a warehouse street, but as a result of redevelopment, offices and galleries have steadily advanced into the quarter. The restaurant, which has been redecorated from a printing house, emphasizes the warehouse atmosphere by effectively introducing the bricked wall, concrete floor, aluminum duct, etc. Thus, the interior finish gives a more high tech and up-beat sense. The menu was eclectic — mixing French cuisine (main) with modern ingredients. The restaurant is closed now.

● AMÉRIQUE (Chicago)
Closed now;　　　Opened/September 1985; Number of seats/90 (restaurant 75, bar 15); Number of employees/25

(Photo captions)
1 / The wall design composed of cloth; periodically changed by a designer.
2 / The high tech sense bar area and dining area whose interior employs aluminum ducts.
3 / The entrance and the bar corner accented with large columns; the reception is visible on the right side.

1/布で構成した壁面のデザイン
2/アルミのダクトもインテリアに取り入れられた　ハイテック感覚のバーエリアとダイニングエリア
3/エントランスと大きな円柱を生かしたバーコーナー　右はレセプション

「アメリーク」はシカゴ河の北　リバーノース(River North)に位置する。この地域は倉庫街だったが再開発により　オフィスやギャラリーが進出している。印刷工場だった建物を改装したこの店は　倉庫の雰囲気を生かし　煉瓦の壁やコンクリートの床　アルミのダクトなどを効果的にインテリアに取り入れ　ハイテック感覚のよりアップビートな感じに仕上げている。メニューはフランス料理をベースに近代的なものをミックスした　エクレクティックな料理を提供していたが　現在は閉店している。

● アメリーク〈シカゴ〉
現在閉店中　開店/1985年9月　客席数/90席(レストラン75席　バー15席)　従業員数/25人

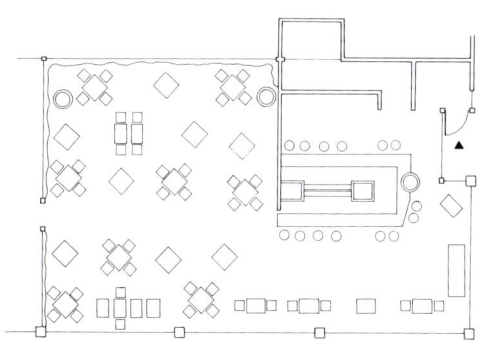

690 SPEEDO ⟨San Francisco⟩

An ethnic restaurant opened on Van Ness Avenue, San Francisco, by Mr. Jeremiah Tower, one of the representative chefs in America, "690 SPEEDO" mainly serves resort seafoods which are available in India, Thailand, Fiji, Morocco, etc. Utilizing a redecorated car repair shop, the interior has a tropical atmosphere and 2/3 of 180-seated guest space is occupied by the bar area whose high ceiling is decorated with an impressive 165-foot painting of resort beach by Philip Core. Intended for guests who are 25 to 35 years old.

● 690 SPEEDO (San Francisco)
Address/690 Van Ness Avenue San Francisco, CA. 94102
Phone/415-255-6900
Opened/May 1989;   Number of seats/180;
Number of employees/80

アメリカにおける代表的なシェフの一人　ジェレミア タワー(Jeremiah Tower)氏が　サンフランシスコのバンネス大通り(Van Ness Avenue)に開店したエスニックレストランでインド タイ フィジー モロッコなど リゾート地のシーフードをメインにした料理を提供している。車の修理工場を改装した店内は　トロピカルな雰囲気のインテリアで　180席の客席の2/3をバーエリアが占め　高い天井空間に飾られたフィリップ コア(Philip Core)の165フィートのリゾートビーチをテーマにした絵が印象的。25～35歳の客層をターゲットにしている。

●スピード 690 〈サンフランシスコ〉
Address/690 Van Ness Avenue San Francisco, CA.94102　Phone/415-255-6900　開店/1989年5月　客席数/180席　従業員数/80人

(Photo captions)
1 / The telephone booths and parasols placed between the bar counter and dining tables image a resort beach.
2 / The 1st floor viewed from the dining area on the 2nd floor.
3 / 2/3 of the wide interior space (redecorated car repair shop) is occupied by the bar corner.

1/バーカウンターとダイニングテーブルの間に置かれた電話ボックスやパラソルが　リゾートビーチのイメージを演出している。
2/2階ダイニングフロアから1階をみる
3/車の修理工場を改装した広い店内は　2/3がバーコーナーで占められている

PIPELINE 〈New York〉

An American food restaurant situated within the office building "The World Financial Center" on an area dubbed "Battery Park City" at the westernmost end of downtown Manhattan. Designed by Sam Lopata, the interior space uniquely images an oil refinery. It introduces an oil storage tank and pipe ducts, while the counter and service areas use metallic finish, striking colors, a TV screen and other ultra-fashionable elements. Managed by Mr. Larry Parish and Daniel Rudolph, "PIPELINE" is mostly visited by businessmen, but on the weekend it is crowded with community inhabitants, Sunday brunch customers, etc.
● PIPELINE (New York)
Address/225 Liberty Street, 2 World Financial Center, New York, N.Y. 10281
Phone/212-945-2755
Opened/July 1989;　Number of seats/140 (restaurant 125, bar counter 15, terrace 130 added in summer time)

マンハッタンのダウンタウンの最西端　別名 "バッテリー パーク シティ" と呼ばれる場所のオフィスビル 「ザ ワールド フィナンシャル センター」内にあるアメリカ料理レストラン。サム ロパタ (Sam Lopata) のデザインでオイル製油所をテーマにしたユニークな空間をつくり出している。店内に油の貯蔵タンクやパイプダクトを持ち込み、カウンター部やサービスエリアにはメタルを使用し　強烈な配色とTVスクリーンを導入するなど　最先端の感覚をとりいれている。経営は Larry Parish 氏と Daniel Rudolph 氏で　ビジネス客の利用が圧倒的だが　週末には周辺の住民やサンデー ブランチなどの客で賑わう。
●パイプライン〈ニューヨーク〉
Address/225 Liberty Street, 2 World Financial Center, New York, N.Y.10281　Phone/212-945-2755　開店/1989年7月　客席数/140席(レストラン125席　バーカウンター15席――夏季には別にテラス 130席あり)

(Photo captions)
1 / Designed by imaging an oil refinery as its theme, many naked pipes cross over the ceiling, thus giving a high tech sense to the interior.
2 / The open bar corner and table seating area are integrated in a colorful and casual atmosphere.

1/製油所をテーマにデザインされたこのレストランは　天井部にむき出しのパイプが縦横に走りハイテックなインテリアで構成されている
2/カラフルでカジュアルな雰囲気の店内は　オープンなバーコーナーとテーブル席が一体になっている

BISTANGO 〈Irvine, CA.〉

Using a coinage made by combining bistro and tango as its name, "BISTANGO" is located in Irvine City, South California. Based on Italian foods, new-style cuisine also incorporating French and Japanese elements is served. The interior designed by Michael Carapetian gives a modern, high tech sense. The dining area utilizes the wide space with a multiple variation, while the open kitchen is placed so that guests can enjoy viewing what's going on there.

● BISTANGO (Irvine, CA.)
Address/19100 Von Karman Avenue Irvine, CA. 92715
Phone/714-752-5222;
Opened/November 1987; Number of seats/ 250 (restaurant 180, bar 70); Number of employees/75

(Photo captions)
1 / The open table seating area accented with cactuses.
2 / The bar corner; with the marbled counter top.
3 / The bar corner area; uniquely accented with the red triangular wine cellar.
4 / The modern dining room; with bamboos introduced into an area by the window through which natural light streams in.
5 / The restaurant is situated on the 1st floor of this office building.

1/カクタスが置かれ 開放的なテーブル席
2/バーコーナー カウンタートップは大理石
3/バーコーナー方向をみる 三角形の赤いワインセラーがユニーク
4/モダン感覚のダイニングルーム 自然光の入る窓際には竹が植え込まれている
5/このオフィスビルの1階にレストランはある

ビストロとタンゴを合わせた造語が店名になっている「ビスタンゴ」は 南カリフォルニアのアーバイン(Irvine)市にある。イタリア料理をベースに 日本的なフランス料理を盛り込んだ新しいスタイルの料理を提供している。インテリアは Michael Carapetianで モダンなハイテク感覚のデザインになっている。ダイニングエリアは マルチプルに変化をつけて広がりを生かし オープンキッチンを設け調理場の動きを見せる演出をしている。

●ビスタンゴ〈カリフォルニア・アーバイン〉
Address/19100 Von Karman Avenue Irvine, CA. 92715 Phone/714-752-5222 開店/1987年11月 客席数/250席(レストラン180席 バー70席) 従業員数/75人

②

④

③

⑤

STELLA'S PLACE 〈Chicago〉

A brasserie managed by Mr. John Stoltzman, a chef in Chicago, "STELLA'S PLACE" offers various types of appetizer, reasonable prices with a la carte system, and an interesting collection of wine — these constitute the shop concept. The interior was designed by Mr. John Cannon who is active mainly in Chicago. He created a female character named "Stella" in order to give personality to the restaurant. The interior space is segmented into three corners, each having a different feeling — an informal lounge bar, an atrium dining room accented with neoned wall paintings of musical instruments, and an inner room decorated with a painted story of Stella in a quiet and affectionate atmosphere. The restaurant is closed now.

● STELLA'S PLACE (Chicago)
Closed now; Opened/June 1986; Number of seats/278 (dining 180, terrace 40, bar 58); Number of employees/25

①

シカゴのシェフ ジョン ストルツマン (John Stoltzman)氏のブラスリー。アペタイザーの種類を多くし ア ラ カルト方式で手頃な価格 興味のあるワインのコレクションがコンセプトのレストランである。
インテリアはシカゴを中心に活躍する John Cannon氏で "レストラン自身にパーソナリティを持たせよう" という発想で ステラという女性をキャラクターとして創り出した。3つのコーナーに分けられた店内は それぞれ異なったフィーリングを持ち インフォーマルなロングバー ネオンの楽器のウォールアートがあるアトリウム ダイニングルーム そして静かで親しみのあるステラの物語が飾られた奥の部屋で構成されている。このレストランは現在閉店されている。

●ステラズ プレイス〈シカゴ〉
現在閉店中 開店/1986年6月 客席数/278席（ダイニング180席 テラス40席 バー58席）従業員数/25人

②

(Photo captions)
1 / The table seating corner featuring wall paintings of Stella's story.
2 / Impressively accented with the mirror top bar counter and neoned clock.
3 / The atrium dining room featuring the large wall art of neoned musical instruments.

1/ステラの人生物語を描いた壁画があるテーブル席
2/ミラートップのバーカウンターとネオンの時計が印象的
3/ネオンの楽器で構成された大きなウォールアートがあるアトリウム ダイニングルーム

SPAGO CALIFORNIA CUISINE ⟨Los Angeles⟩

Mainly used by people involved in the film industry, elites, etc. in Hollywood, Los Angeles, "SPAGO" is a Californian cuisine restaurant managed by Mr. Wolfgang Pack, one of the representative American chefs. The menu covers a wide range of foods from popular pastas and pizzas to French cuisine, but is limited to 25 items from appetizer to dessert. The interior was designed by female designer Barbara Lazaroff who is a partner and friend of the owner-chef. The artistic finish and contemporary decor create an atmosphere which agrees well with this location in Hollywood.

● SPAGO CALIFORNIA CUISINE
　(Los Angeles)
Address/8795 Sunset Boulevard Los Angeles, CA. 90069
Opened/January 1982; Number of seats/150 (main dining 110, terrace 40); Number of employees/60

ロサンゼルスのハリウッド地区で　映画関係者やエリートたちが集まるこの「スパゴ」は　アメリカを代表するシェフ　ウルフギャング　パック（Wolfgang Pack）氏のカリフォルニア料理レストランである。大衆的なパスタやピザからフランス料理まで幅広い料理を扱っているがアペタイザーからデザートまで25種のアイテムに限定し提供している。インテリアはオーナーシェフのパートナーであり　友人の女性デザイナー　バーバラ　ラザロフ（Barbara Lazaroff）さんで　アーティスティックな作品とコンテンポラリーなデコアが地域にマッチした雰囲気を醸しだしている。

●スパゴ　カリフォルニアキュイジーヌ〈ロサンゼルス〉
Address/8795 Sunset Boulevard Los Angeles, CA.90069　開店/1982年1月　客席数/150席（メインダイニング110席　テラス40席）従業員数/60人

(Photo captions)
1 / The terrace seating area with parasols and objets.
2 / The contemporary main dining room; with the wall art by Barbara Lazaroff.
3 / The elegant dining room agrees well with the atmosphere of Hollywood.

1/パラソルやオブジェの置かれたテラス席
2/コンテンポラリーなメインダイニング　壁面のアートは Barbara Lazaroff さんの作品
3/エレガントなダイニングはハリウッドの持つ雰囲気にマッチしている

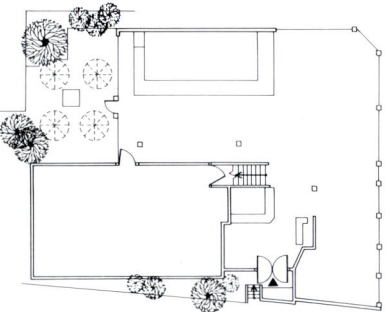

ROBBIN'S ⟨New York⟩

Dishes served at "ROBBIN'S" are called "American bistro" cuisine which is a little refined version of American cuisine. The restaurant is situated on an area which is close to downtown Manhattan and crowded with fashion-related offices, residences, etc. The interior is decorated with objets of contemporary art, etc. Produced by friends of Mr. Robbin, owner, these objets convey the spirit of play and humor. The restaurant is closed now.

● ROBBIN'S (New York)
Closed now; Opened/January 1990; Number of seats/73 (restaurant 60, bar 13); Number of employees/18

「ロビンズ」の料理は　伝統的なアメリカ料理を少し洗練させた"アメリカン ビストロ"と呼ばれるもの。マンハッタンのダウンタウンに近い　ファッション関係のオフィスや住宅が密集する場所に立地している。店内には現代アートのオブジェなどの作品が飾られている。これらはオーナーのロビン氏の友人たちの創作によるもので　遊び心やユーモアを感じさせる。このレストランは現在閉店されている。

●ロビンズ〈ニューヨーク〉
現在閉店中　開店/1990年1月　客席数/73席（レストラン60席　バー13席）　従業員数/18人

(Photo captions)
1 / The bar corner.
2・3 / The dining room whose walls are decorated with a unique objet made by collecting empty detergent bottles, and pieces of contemporary art.

1/バーコーナー
2・3/ダイニング　壁面には洗剤の空瓶を集めたユニークな作品や現代アートが飾られている

TUMBLEWEED 〈Beverly Hills, CA.〉

"TUMBLEWEED" is a restaurant which serves American southern foods cooked in new styles by Ms. Elka Gilmore, female chef born in Texas. Commenting on her dishes, she says: "My dishes are such that guests want to taste them even everyday." She exquisitely combines her own sauce with barbecue or charcoal-baked smoked cooking which is very popular in Texas. Landscape photos displayed on the yellow wall are colored by hand which, together with an objet imaging a farmhouse, are Jane Krensky's works. The restaurant is closed now.
● TUMBLEWEED (Beverly Hills CA.)
Closed now;   Opened/December 1987;
Number of seats/46

テキサス生まれの女性シェフ　ギルモア（Elka Gilmore）さんの新しいスタイルのアメリカの南部料理を提供するレストラン。彼女自身"自分の料理は毎日でも食べたい料理である"といい特にテキサスでよく親しまれているバーベキューや炭焼きでスモークした調理法に　彼女独特のソースを加えて特色を出したもの。店内の黄色い壁面に飾られた田舎の風景写真は　ハンドメイドで着色したもので　農家をイメージしたオブジェ同様　Jane Krenskyの作品。この店は現在閉店中である。
●タンブルウィード〈カリフォルニア・ビバリーヒルズ〉
現在閉店中　開店/1987年12月　客席数/46席

(Photo captions)
1 / The dining room having a casual atmosphere; with a skylight above the inner open kitchen.
2 / The objet imaging a farmhouse; Jane Krensky's art.

1/カジュアルな雰囲気のダイニング　奥のオープンキッチンの上には天窓が配されている
2/農家をイメージしたオブジェ　Jane Krenskyの作品

HARD ROCK CAFE ⟨Los Angeles⟩

Situated on the 1st floor of "Beverly Center," a high-class shopping center in Los Angeles, "HARD ROCK CAFE" employs "fifties" as the store concept. The facade is accented with a calypso green Cadillac made in 1959 which just looks as if running into the roof while winking its tail lamps. In the restaurant where Harley-Davidson once owned by Presley, a racket used by Jimmy Connors when he won the championship at the US Open Tennis, university flags, stuffed buffalo and American lion, etc. are displayed, waitresses in white uniform, which fashioned in the 1950s, are working.

● HARD ROCK CAFE (Los Angeles)
Address/8600 Beverly Boulevard Los Angeles, CA.
Opened/October 1982; Number of seats/180

(Photo captions)
1 / The unique facade on the 1st floor of "Beverly Center."
2 / The interior taking up the 1950s as the design theme.

ロサンゼルスの高級ショッピングセンターの「ビバリー センター（Beverly Center）」の1階にある。店のコンセプトはフィフティーズで ファサードの屋根に突き刺さるように1959年製のカリプソ グリーンのキャデラックが置かれ テールランプがウインクする演出にはじまり 店内には'50年代に流行した 白いユニホーム姿のウエイトレスたちがサービスし プレスリーが愛用していたハーレイ ダビッドソンやジミー コナースがUSオープンテニスで優勝時に使用したラケット 大学の旗 バッファローやアメリカ ライオンの剥製などが飾られている。

●ハード ロック カフェ〈ロサンゼルス〉
Address/8600 Beverly Boulevard Los Angeles, CA． 開店/1982年10月　客席数／180席

1／「ビバリー センター」1階のユニークなファサード
2／1950年代をデザインのテーマにした店内

Restaurant & Bar at MORGANS ⟨New York⟩

Placed at the basement of "Morgans" which is hotly talked about as a boutique hotel, "Restaurant & Bar at MORGANS" features a fusion of dramatic sense and high tech sense. A little purplish grey walls, ceiling whose concrete foundation is exposed, neat tableware on the white tablecloth, stool, sofa and other piece of furniture — all these elements are simply installed and add to the dignified mood.

- Restaurant & Bar at MORGANS (New York)
Address/237 Madison Avenue New York, N.Y. 10016a
Phone/212-686-0300; Opened/October 1984

(Photo captions)
1 / The entrance hall featuring a new design sense.
2 / The dining area; with uniquely arranged tables.

1/新しいデザイン感覚のエントランスホール
2/ダイニングエリア ユニークなテーブル配置になっている

ブティックホテルとして話題の「Morgans」の地下にあり ドラマチックな感覚と ハイテックな感覚を融合させたレストラン。やや紫がかったグレイの壁面と コンクリート打ち放しの天井 白いクロスがかけられたテーブルに並べられた小道具 そしてスツール ソファなどのファニチュアが シンプルな中にも いかにも格調の高いムードを盛り上げている。

● レストラン & バー アット モーガンズ ⟨ニューヨーク⟩
Address/237 Madison Avenue New York, N.Y. 10016a Phone/212-686-0300 開店/1984年10月

SATURNIA ⟨New York⟩

In this restaurant which offers diet foods, every item on the menu comes with the corresponding calorific value and fat point (F.P.). A course ordering system is employed which selects one each from the three categories — appetizer, entrée and dessert — after checking their calorific values and F.P. Instead of lopsided pursuit of diet by, for instance, avoiding meat, the chef uses all types of daily ingredients to prepare dishes which are limited in amount of each ingredient, but balanced and pleasing to the eye. The interior is elegantly designed with Greco-Roman garden frescos on the wall. Designed by Sarah Lee.

● SATURNIA (New York)
Address/54 Varick Street New York, N.Y. 10013
Phone/212-966-1239
Opened/September 1990;   Number of seats/75 (dining 70, bar 5)

ダイエットフードを提供するこのレストランのメニューには　どの料理にもカロリー数と脂肪値（ファット ポイント──F.P.）が記されている。オーダーは　アペタイザー　アントレ　デザートの3つのカテゴリーから各1品を選ぶコース料理を採用し　カロリー　脂肪値がチェックされているのが特徴。料理には日常使用されているあらゆる素材が使用され　肉類を避けるといった片寄ったダイエット志向ではなく　素材の分量を制限し　ボリュームや視覚的にもバランスのとれた満足感を持たせた料理を提供している。インテリアは　壁面にグレコ　ローマン風の庭園が描かれ　エレガントな店づくりになっている。デザインは Sarah Lee。

● サターニア ⟨ニューヨーク⟩
Address/54 Varick Street New York, N.Y. 10013　Phone/212-966-1239　開店/1990年9月　客席数/75席（ダイニング70席　バー5席）

①

②

(Photo captions)
1 / The entrance hall to the restaurant; on the 1st floor of "Doral Park Hotel."
2 / The bar corner; uniformly finished with black & white.
3・4 / The dining room in elegant European style accented with a Greco-Roman garden fresco.
5 / Stresses the expanse by a mirror-finished wall.

1/レストランへのエントランスホール　「Doral Park Hotel」の1階にある
2/バーコーナー　白と黒で統一している
3・4/グレコ　ローマン（Greco Roman）の庭園の壁画があるダイニング　ヨーロッパ調のエレガントな雰囲気
5/壁面にミラーを配し　広がりを強調している

JIM MACMAHON'S ⟨Chicago⟩

"JIM MACMAHON'S" is an American cuisine restaurant which takes up "brilliant memories of the sports world" as its theme. The owner Mr. Jim McMahon is a famous football player who once played an active part in the "Chicago Bears." The interior is decorated with many photos and a collection of uniform. Thus, the restaurant is frequently visited by his fans and ordinary sports fans. It is composed of a bar and dining room on the 1st floor and a banquet room named "Press Club" on the basement.
● JIM MACMAHON'S (Chicago)
Address/1970 North Lincoln Avenue Chicago, Illinois 60614
Phone/312-751-1700
Opened/April 1987;   Number of seats/332 (bar & dining 242, banquet room 90)

"スポーツ界の輝かしい思い出"をテーマにしたシカゴのアメリカ料理レストランで オーナーのジム マクマホン(Jim Macmahon)氏は〈シカゴ ベアーズ〉で活躍した有名なフットボールプレイヤーで 店内には数々の写真やユニホームのコレクションが飾られている。彼のファンやスポーツ愛好者がよく訪れる。1階はバーとダイニング 地階は〈プレスクラブ〉と名付けたバンケットルームになっている。
●ジム マクマホンズ〈シカゴ〉
Address/1970 North Lincoln Avenue Chicago, Illinois 60614   Phone/312-751-1700   開店/1987年4月   客席数/332席(バー&ダイニング242席 バンケットルーム90席)

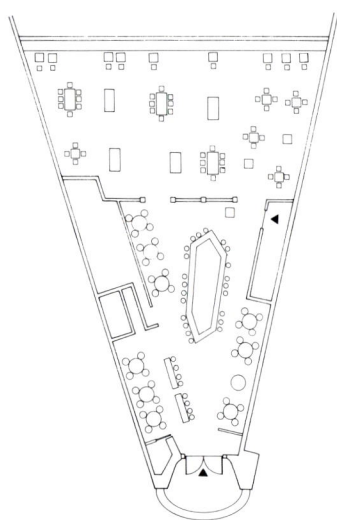

(Photo captions)
1 / The facade; V-shaped by utilizing a corner of Lincoln Avenue.
2 / The bar corner having a pub-like atmosphere.
3 / The toilet uses red & white tiles to stress cleanliness.
4 / The wooden floored dining area whose walls are decorated with photos and uniform collection.

1/Lincoln アベニューの角を利用したV字型のファサード
2/パブ感覚のバーコーナー
3/トイレには赤と白のタイルを用いて明るさを強調している
4/木製フロアのダイニングエリア 壁面には写真やユニフォームのコレクションが飾られている

POSTRIO RESTAURANT ⟨San Francisco⟩

A restaurant jointly opened by Mr. Wolfgang Puck, owner-chef of "Spago" (see page 146), and Mr. and Mrs. David and Anne Gingrass who once served as chefs at "Spago's." The design was undertaken by Mr. Pat Kuleto. The interior space has 3 levels and is composed of a bar corner on the street level, a semibasement and a dining area at the basement. 4-color ribbon patterns crawl across the carpet and marble floor, thus giving uniform images to all floors. The menu is mainly composed of classic San Franciscan foods and dishes which utilize local ingredients.
● POSTRIO RESTAURANT (San Francisco)
Address/545 Post Street San Francisco, CA. 94102
Phone/415-776-7825
Opened/April 1989;   Number of seats/180 (restaurant 150, bar 30);   Number of employees/90

あの「スパゴ(Spago)」(本書146ページ収録)のオーナー シェフ Wolfgang Puck氏と同店でシェフをつとめた Anne and David Gingrass夫妻が 共同で始めたレストランである。デザインは Pat Kuleto氏で 3層からなる店内はストリート レベルのバーコーナー 中地下とその下のダイニングエリアで構成されている。4色のリボンのパターンがカーペットや大理石のフロアを這い 各フロアの統一感を表している。料理はクラシックなサンフランシスコ地方の料理やローカルな食材を生かしたものを提供している。
●ポストリオ レストラン〈サンフランシスコ〉
Address/545 Post Street San Francisco, CA. 94102 Phone/415-776-7825 開店/1989年4月
客席数/180席(レストラン150席 バー30席)
従業員数/90名

①

②

(Photo captions)
1 / The dining area on the semibasement; the wall is decorated with objets whose motif is restaurant scenery.
2 / The service bar beside the central staircase in the main dining area; the staircase's handrails are also provided with ribbon patterns.
3 / The main dining area; uniquely accented with ribbon patterns crawling upon the floor and round lighting appliances.

1/中地下のダイニングエリア 壁面にはレストランをモチーフにしたオブジェが飾られている
2/メインダイニングの中央階段脇のサービスバー 階段の手摺りにもリボンのパターンが施されている
3/メインダイニング フロアを這うリボンのパターンと円形の照明がユニーク

OUT TAKES 〈Chicago〉

Subtitled "Gallery Bar Restaurant," "OUT TAKES" is a restaurant in Chicago which mainly serves cold dishes. The interior space layout is such that it looks as if a bar and restaurant have been brought into a photo display space where the works of contemporary photographers are actually displayed and sold. The name "Out Takes" means that, after choosing the best among photos taken, all others are discarded. The interior space is composed of a 120-seated bar corner and table seating area. The bar counter is uniquely equipped with a glazed water container in which tropical fish are swimming. Frequented by middle-aged professionals and those engaged in creative work.
● OUT TAKES (Chicago)
Address/16 West Ontario Chicago, Illinois 60610
Phone/312-951-7979
Opened/February 1987;   Number of seats/120 (restaurant 40, bar 80)

"ギャラリー バー レストラン"というサブタイトルをつけたシカゴのコールド ディッシュがメインのレストラン。写真作品の展示場内にバーとレストランを持ち込んだような店内構成になっており 現代写真家の作品の展示 販売をしている。店名の「アウト テイクス」は 撮影済みの写真のうち最も良い作品を残し 他は捨て去るという意味からつけられた。店内は120席のバーコーナーとテーブル席で構成され バーカウンターは水槽になっており 熱帯魚が泳ぐユニークな造りになっている。ミドルエイジのプロフェッショナルやクリエイティブな仕事に携わる人たちが客層。
●アウト テイクス〈シカゴ〉
Address/16 West Ontario Chicago, Illinois 60610 Phone/312-951-7979 開店/1987年2月 客席数/120席(レストラン40席 バー80席)

①

②

(Photo captions)
1 / The counter with a water container, photos and music are features of this restaurant.
2 / The restaurant is situated at the basement of a building having an artistic facade.
3 / The gallery-style bar corner which also serves as a place for exhibiting and selling photos taken by contemporary photographers.

1/水槽のカウンターと写真作品 そして音楽がうりものの店内
2/アーティスティックなファーサードの建物の地下にある
3/現代写真作家の作品展と販売をかねるギャラリー風のバーコーナー

GORDON 〈Chicago〉

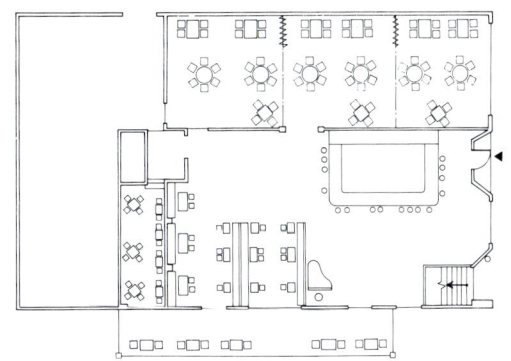

A restaurant serving new-type American foods cooked with less salt, butter, etc. According to Mr. Gordon Sinclir, owner-chef, his motto is "health, nutrition and beautiful dishing up." The interior, which images a theater in the suburbs of Rome, is decorated with frescos by a Chicagoan female artist, and uses materials such as ceramic tiles, rosewood, latten and marble, thereby creating an informal but elegant atmosphere.
● GORDON (Chicago)
Address/500 North Clark Street Chicago, Illinois 60610
Phone/312-467-9780
Opened/December 1984;   Number of seats/140;   Number of employees/60

塩分やバターを控えて調理した 新しいアメリカ料理を提供するレストラン。オーナー シェフのゴードン シンクレア (Gordon Sinclir) 氏のモットーは健康と栄養 美しい盛り付けだという。ローマ郊外の劇場をイメージしたインテリアの店内は シカゴの女性アーティストを起用した壁画やセラミックタイル ローズウッド ラタン マーブルなどの材質で構成され インフォーマルな中にもエレガントな雰囲気が創りだされている。
●ゴードン〈シカゴ〉
Address/500 North Clark Street Chicago, Illinois 60610　Phone/312-467-9780　開店/1984年12月　客席数/140席　従業員数/60名

(Photo captions)
1 / The wall finish with frescos by a Chicagoan female artist is another pride of this restaurant.
2 / The dining area designed after a Roman theatrical image.
3 / The bar corner.

1/女性アーティストを起用した壁面構成はこのレストランの自慢のひとつ
2/ローマの劇場風インテリアのダイニングエリア
3/バーコーナー

ST. JAMES'S CLUB ⟨Los Angeles⟩

"ST. JAMES'S CLUB" is a club style hotel opened in Los Angeles by redecorating an apartment house called the "Sunset Tower" which faces Sunset Boulevard. The main dining room "The Member's Dining Room" and the bar lounge "The Club Bar & Lounge" are open only to the club members and their guests. The menu offered by the chef Gary Clauson is mainly composed of contemporary French and Californian cuisine. The architectural design was undertaken by David L. Gray & Associates, and the interior design by David Becker.

● ST. JAMES'S CLUB (Los Angeles)
Address/8358 Sunset Boulevard Los Angeles, CA. 90069
Phone/213-654-7100
Opened/March 1988;   Number of seats/120 (restaurant 80, bar 40)

ロサンゼルスのサンセット大通り(Sunset Boulevard)に面した サンセットタワーと呼ばれるアパートメントを改装してクラブ式のホテルがオープン。メインダイニングの「The Member's Dining Room」とバーラウンジ「The Club Bar & Lounge」は 会員とそのゲストのみに開放される。シェフのゲリィ クローソン(Gary Clauson)氏の提供するメニューは コンテンポラリーなフランスとカリフォルニア料理が中心となっている。設計は建築 David L.Gray & Associates インテリアは David Becker。

●セント ジェイムス クラブ ⟨ロサンゼルス⟩
Address/8358 Sunset Boulevard Los Angeles, CA.90069 Phone/213-654-7100 開店/1988年3月 客席数/120席(レストラン80席 バー40席)

(Photo captions)
1 / "The Club Bar & Lounge" having an art deco atmosphere.
2 / The entrance.
3 / The elegant dining room in which light streams through the skylight.

1/アートデコの雰囲気を持つ「The Club Bar & Lounge」
2/エントランス
3/スカイライトが入るエレガントなダイニングルーム

CITY GRILL ⟨Los Angeles⟩

A restaurant situated in "Hilton & Towers" downtown Los Angeles, "CITY GRILL" mainly serves lunch. Using greyish rose as its theme color which is accented with emerald green, the interior features an elegant atmosphere of modern art deco. The menu is composed of selected items which are popular as special or seasonal foods. After the lunchtime, the restaurant changes into a cocktail lounge serving tapas dishes as hors d'œuvre, and is fully intended for business guests. There is no dinner service.

● CITY GRILL (Los Angeles)
Address/Los Angeles Hilton & Towers, 930 Wilshire Boulevard Los Angeles, CA. 90017
Phone/213-623-5971
Opened/July 1987; Number of guests/147; Number of employees/19

(Photo captions)
1 / The modern art deco facade.
2 / The dining room and open banquet room.
3 / The dining area; laid out according to the round bar counter in the center.

ロサンゼルスのダウンタウンの「ヒルトン＆タワーズ」の中にある ランチを主体としたレストラン。テーマカラーのグレイッシュ ローズにエメラルド グリーンでアクセントを持たせた店内は モダンアートデコのエレガントな雰囲気となっている。料理はアイテムをしぼりスペシャルメニューとして 人気のある料理や季節感のある料理を加えている。ランチタイムのあとは パスタ料理をオードブルとして提供するカクテルラウンジになり 完全にビジネス客を対象にしている。ディナーの営業はない。

●シティ グリル ⟨ロサンゼルス⟩
Address/Los Angeles Hilton & Towers, 930 Wilshire Boulevard Los Angeles, CA.90017
Phone/213-623-5971 開店/1987年7月 客席数/147席 従業員数/19人

1/モダンアートデコのファサード
2/ダイニングルームと開放的なバンケットルーム
3/ダイニングエリア 中央 円形のバーカウンターに合わせレイアウトされている

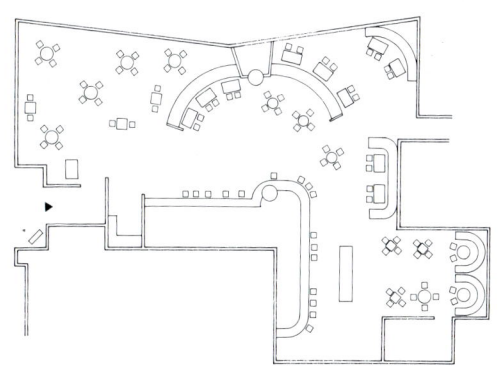

MUSTANG GRILL 〈New York〉

"MUSTANG GRILL" is another name of wild horses which are found in Mexico, the Southwest of America, etc. The menu offered by the chef Michael Kimmel blends Tex-Mex and basic American foods in New England. The interior was designed by imaging the strong sunlight and desert in the Southwest. The center wall is decorated with a painting of armadillo, cowboy and skyline of Manhattan, New York, drawn by artist Paul Bianiz — another Tex-Mex expression. Although the restaurant had drawn attention as a new spot in New York, it is closed now.
● MUSTANG GRILL (New York)
Closed now; Opened/November 1990; Number of seats/104 (restaurant 90, bar 14)

店名の「マスタング グリル」は メキシコやアメリカの西南部で見られる野生馬の別称。シェフのマイケル キンメル(Michael Kimmel)氏による料理は テックス メックスとニューイングランドのベーシックなアメリカ料理をブレンドしたメニュー。店内は西南部の強い陽射しと砂漠をイメージしたインテリアで 中央部にはアーティストのポール ビアニッツ(Paul Bianiz)氏のアルマジロ カウボーイとニューヨークのマンハッタンのスカイラインを描いた絵画があり ここにもテックス メックスが表現されている。この店はニューヨークの新しいスポットとして注目されていたが 現在閉店している。
●マスタング グリル〈ニューヨーク〉
現在閉店中 開店/1990年11月 客席数/104席
(レストラン90席 バー14席)

①

②

③

④

(Photo captions)
1・5 / The dining room; imaging the strong sunlight and desert in the Southwest.
2 / The bar area; reminds us of a saloon in the Southwest.
3 / The wall painting was drawn by Mr. Paul Bianiz.
4 / The staircase area; accented with interesting handrail curves.

1・5/ダイニングルーム 西南部の強い陽射しと砂漠をイメージしている
2/バーエリア 西南部のサルーンを思わせる
3/壁面の絵画はポール ビアニッツ(Paul Bianiz)氏の作品
4/階段廻り 手摺りの曲線がおもしろい

555 EAST ⟨Long Beach, CA.⟩

Facing the sea, "555 EAST" is a traditional New York style bar & restaurant situated on a Long Beach business street, and mainly serves seafoods. The dining area having a composed atmosphere with dark green walls and brass rods. With "Guest First" as its motto, the restaurant serves dishes using fresh ingredients.

● 555 EAST (Long Beach, CA.)
Address/555 East Ocean Boulevard Long Beach, CA. 90802
Phone/213-497-0626
Opened/May 1984;   Number of seats/155 (restaurant 120, bar 35);   Number of employees/75

(Photo captions)
1 / The dining room in the traditional New York style; the green wall finish gives a composed impression.
2 / The facade.
3 / The bar area; at lunchtime, opened for eating.

海に面したロングビーチのビジネス街にある伝統的なニューヨークスタイルのバーとレストランで シーフードに力を入れている。ダークグリーンの壁面にブラスのロッドを配し 落着いた雰囲気のダイニングで "お客様第一=guest first" をモットーにフレッシュな食材を使用した料理を提供している。

●555 イースト 〈カリフォルニア・ロングビーチ〉

Address/555 East Ocean Boulevard Long Beach, CA.90802 Phone/213-497-0626 開店/1984年5月 客席数/155席(レストラン120席 バー35席) 従業員数/75人

1/伝統的なニューヨークスタイルのダイニングルーム グリーンの壁面で落着いた雰囲気
2/ファサード
3/バーエリア ランチタイムには食事用に開放される

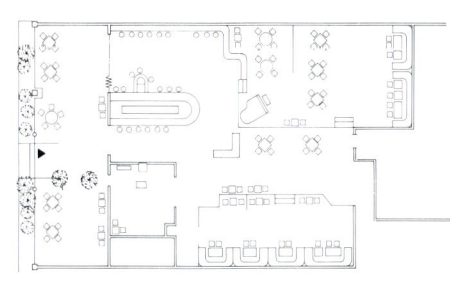

カジュアル & ディナーレストラン-2

- ザ ブッチャー ショップ〈シカゴ〉 174
- ザ アヴェニュー グリル〈カリフォルニア・ミル ヴァレイ〉 176
- ビストロ 110〈シカゴ〉 178
- ザ リッツ カフェ〈ロサンゼルス〉 180
- キャンプトン プレイス〈サンフランシスコ〉 182
- ウィンドーズ オン ザ ワールド〈ニューヨーク〉 184
- ダン ロス リバープラザ〈シカゴ〉 186
- モーベンピック〈ニューヨーク〉 188
- ブラボー フォノ〈カリフォルニア・パロ アルト〉 190
- ズッキーニ〈テキサス・ダラス〉 192
- ザ ピンク ベアー〈ジョージア・アトランタ〉 193
- ランガンズ ブラッセリー〈ロサンゼルス〉 194
- ザ ベルベット タートル〈カリフォルニア・シティ オブ インダストリー〉 196
- ラスティ スカッパー〈サンフランシスコ〉 198
- クック ブック〈カリフォルニア・エルトロ〉 200
- フォーティ キャロッツ〈カリフォルニア・トーランス〉 202
- レインボー ビア フィッシュ マーケット〈カリフォルニア・ロングビーチ〉 204
- ビクトリア ステーション〈カリフォルニア・ユニバーサル シティ〉 206
- ティ ビー カプランズ〈シカゴ〉 208
- レッド ロビン〈カリフォルニア・ロス アラミトス〉 210
- オーガン グラインダー〈コロラド・デンバー〉 212
- ハムレット ガーデンズ〈ロサンゼルス〉 214

Casual & Dinner restaurants-2

THE BUTCHER SHOP ⟨Chicago⟩ 174
THE AVENUE GRILL ⟨Mill Valley, CA.⟩ 176
BISTRO 110 ⟨Chicago⟩ 178
THE RITZ CAFE ⟨Los Angeles⟩ 180
CAMPTON PLACE ⟨San Francisco⟩ 182
WINDOW ON THE WORLD ⟨New York⟩ 184
DON ROTH'S RIVER PLAZA ⟨Chicago⟩ 186
MÖVENPIC ⟨New York⟩ 188
BRAVO FONO ⟨Palo Alto, CA.⟩ 190
ZUCCHINI'S ⟨Dallas, Texas⟩ 192
THE PINK PEAR ⟨Atlanta, Georgia⟩ 193
LANGAN'S BRASSERIE ⟨Los Angeles⟩ 194
THE VELVET TURTLE ⟨City of Industry, CA.⟩ 196
RUSTY SCUPPER ⟨San Francisco⟩ 198
COOK BOOK ⟨El Toro, CA.⟩ 200
FORTY CARROTS ⟨Tarrance, CA.⟩ 202
RAINBOW PIER FISH MARKET ⟨Long Beach, CA.⟩ 204
VICTORIA STATION ⟨Universal City, CA.⟩ 206
D.B. KAPLAN'S ⟨Chicago⟩ 208
RED ROBIN ⟨Los Alamitos, CA.⟩ 210
ORGAN GRINDER ⟨Denver, Colorado⟩ 212
HAMLET GARDENS ⟨Los Angeles⟩ 214

THE BUTCHER SHOP 〈Chicago〉

A steak restaurant situated in River North, downtown Chicago. This restaurant employs a unique service concept — any of five types of meat (including fillet minion and top sirloin) is served at a fixed price of $15.15 with a different weight. The interior makeup has a casual, rustic atmosphere, and is decorated with paintings whose theme is Chicago.
● THE BUTCHER SHOP (Chicago)
Address/358 West Ontario Chicago, Illinois 60610
Phone/312-440-4900
Opened/October 1987; Number of employees/70〜80

(Photo captions)
1 / The full-service bar featuring a collection of many bottles.
2 / The dining area featuring a casual, rustic make-up.
3 / The facade; situated downtown Chicago.

1/フルサービスバー　数多いボトルのコレクションが自慢
2/カジュアルな田舎風造りのダイニングエリア
3/ファサード　シカゴのダウンタウンに位置している

シカゴのダウンタウン　リバー　ノース(River North)地区にあるステーキレストラン。この店のユニークなコンセプトは　フィレミニオン　トップサーロインなど5種類の肉を　それぞれ異なった重さで　価格を統一(15.15ドル)し提供していることである。店内はカジュアルな田舎風の造りでシカゴをテーマにした絵画が飾られている。
●ザ　ブッチャー　ショップ〈シカゴ〉
Address/358 West Ontario Chicago, Illinois 60610
Phone/312-440-4900　開店/1987年10月　従業員/70〜80人

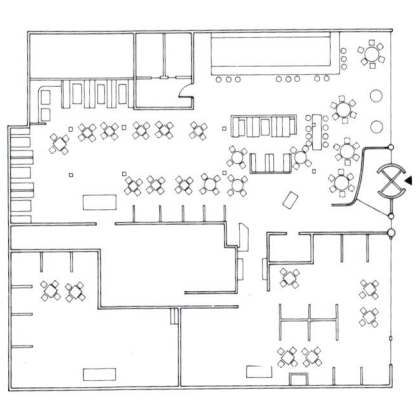

②

③

THE AVENUE GRILL 〈Mill Valley, CA.〉

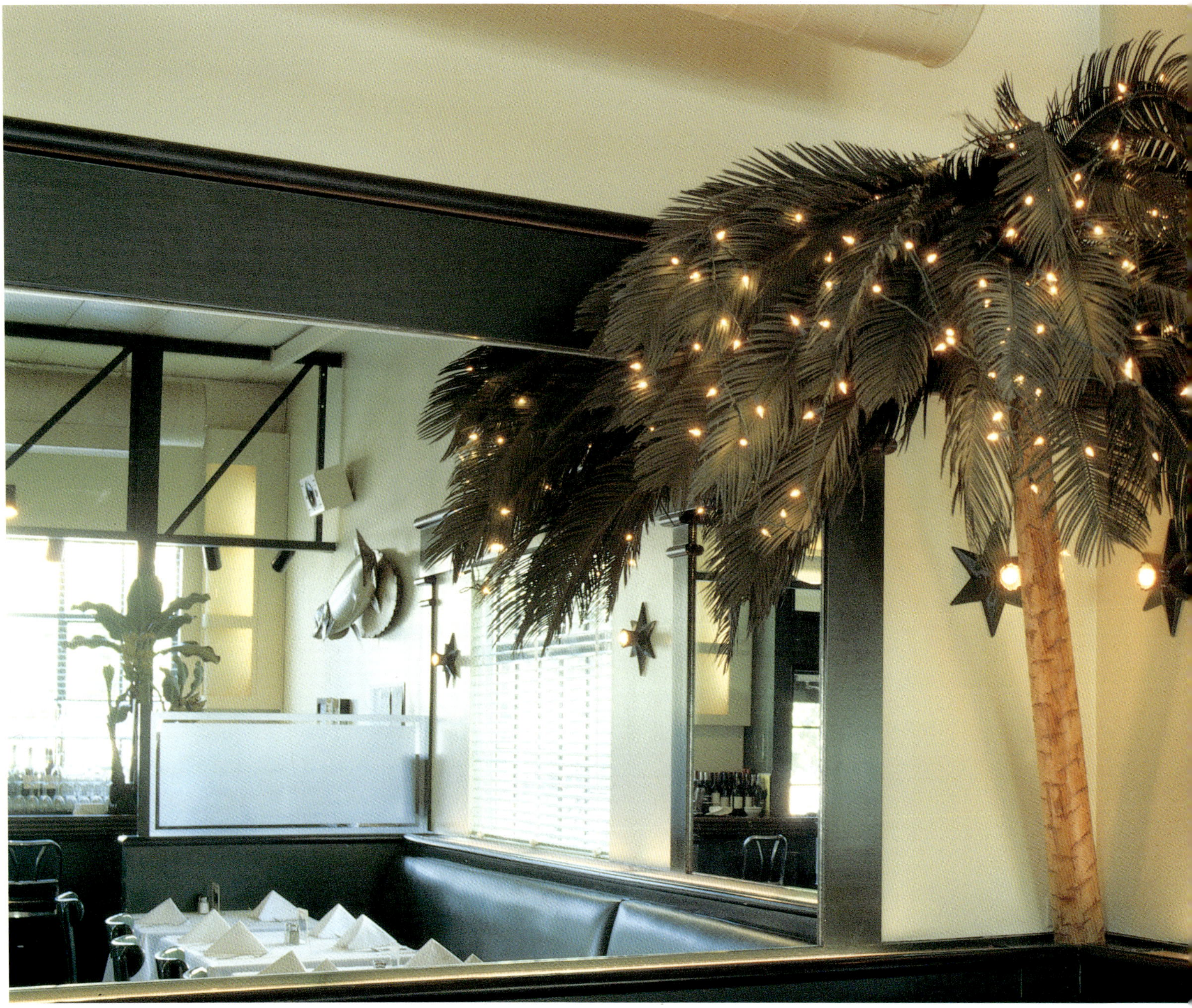

②

③

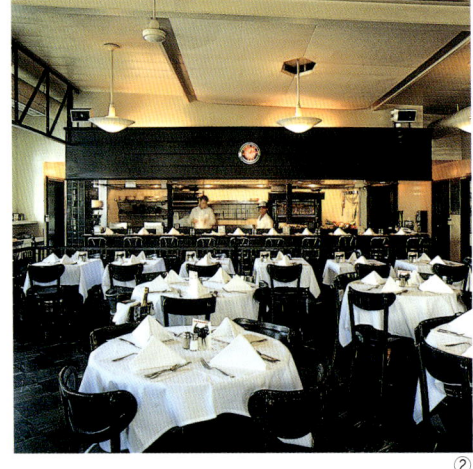

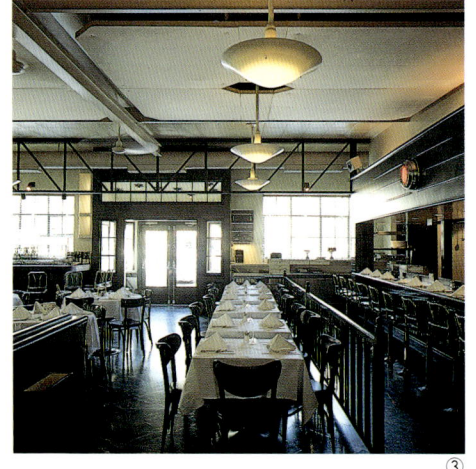

An American ethnic restaurant situated in Mill Valley which is 7 to 8 miles (about 10 km) away from San Francisco across the Golden Gate Bridge. Here, meat loaf, pasta and roast chicken are among the popular menu items. The building was originally a gas station which was later redecorated into the existing restaurant. According to Ms. Marni Leis, owner and designer, it was her intention to create an image — "Although it is a new space, it has always existed there since a long time ago." Starting with the 1930s art deco, the interior design has continued to change its image in a series through the '40s, '50s and '60s, in turn. All items are reasonably priced at this restaurant which is open only for dinner.

● THE AVENUE GRILL (Mill Valley, CA.)
Address/44 E. Bithedale Mill Valley, CA. 94941
Phone/415-388-6003
Opened/September 1985; Number of seats/87 (table 76, counter 11); Number of employees/35

サンフランシスコのゴールデン ゲイト ブリッジを渡り7〜8マイル(約10km)のミル ヴァレイに位置するアメリカン エスニックのレストランで ミートローフやパスタ料理 チキンのローストなどに人気がある。元はガソリンスタンドだった建物を改装したもの。オーナーでデザイナーのMarni Leisさんは 新しいスペースであるが"ずっと以前からいつもそこにあったレストラン"というイメージ造りをしたという。デザインはアートデコで 開店当初は1930年代の雰囲気で 以後40年 50年 60年代の雰囲気へとデザインをシリーズ化して変化させてきている。リーズナブルな価格設定で ディナーのみの営業となっている。

●ジ アヴェニュー グリル〈カリフォルニア・ミル ヴァレイ〉
Address/44 E.Bithedale Mill Valley,CA.94941
Phone/415-388-6003 開店/1985年9月 客席数/87席(テーブル76席 カウンター11席) 従業員数/35名

(Photo captions)
1 / The wall mirror gives an expansive impression.
2 / The dining area equipped with an open kitchen.
3 / Art deco elements are introduced even into the lighting equipment and chairs along the counter.
4 / The facade; formerly, the building was a gas station.

1/壁面のミラーが広さを演出している
2/オープンキッチンを備えたダイニングエリア
3/照明やカウンター席の椅子にもアートデコが取り入れられている
4/ファサード 元はガソリンスタンドだった

BISTRO 110 ⟨Chicago⟩

A casual restaurant situated at a corner of Water Tower Place in Chicago which is visited by many tourists, "BISTRO 110" has a traditional European bistro-like atmosphere. In the restaurant, a glassed sidewalk is provided, a warm atmosphere is stressed by contemporary lighting appliances and pine-wood floor, and the walls are decorated with frescos painted by artist Judy Rifka. The menu includes many items which are roasted and flavored with garlic, thyme and various types of herb.

● BISTRO 110 (Chicago)
Address/110 East Peason Street Chicago, Illinois 60611
Phone/312-266-3110
Opened/October 1987; Number of seats/195

(Photo captions)
1 / The interior space with contemporary lighting appliances; the booth seating and dining areas are placed on different levels.
2 / The dining area whose walls are decorated with judy Rifka's frescos.
3 / The booth seats corner.
4 / The facade; provided with a glassed sidewalk cafe.

シカゴの観光客が集まるウォーター タワー プレイス(Water Tower Place)の一角にあるカジュアルで ヨーロッパの伝統的なビストロの雰囲気を持つレストラン。ガラス張りのサイドウォークカフェが設けられ コンテンポラリーな照明器具と松材のフロアで温かさを強調した店内には アーティストJudy Rifkaの壁画が飾られている。ローストし ガーリックやタイム ハーブ類の香りを強調した料理が多い。

● ビストロ 110 ⟨シカゴ⟩
Address/110 East Peason Street Chicago, Illinois 60611 Phone/312-266-3110 開店/1987年10月 客席数/195席

①

THE RITZ CAFE ⟨Los Angeles⟩

Situated near Beverly Hills, "THE RITZ CAFE" is a "Cajun·Creloe" food restaurant. Originated mainly in South Louisiana, those dishes have been created by immigrants from South France in the mid 18th century. Influenced by African-Louisianan taste, "Cajun" cuisine is French countryside foods which use various kinds of seasoning and pepper. "Creole" cuisine, on the other hand, features an urban taste, influenced mainly by French, Spanish, African and Indian tastes, and are less spicy than "Cajun." The interior is simply designed to introduce natural light from the ceiling into the central part of the dining area, while booth seats are also installed. The restaurant is closed now.
● THE RITZ CAFE (Los Angeles)
Closed now; Opened/June 1984; Number of seats/162 (restaurant 150, bar 12); Number of employees/80

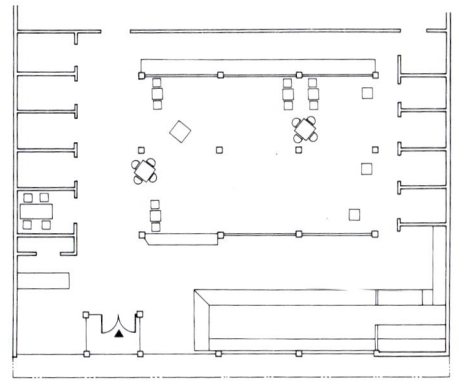

ビバリーヒルズの近くに位置する"ケイジャン (Cajun)""クレオール(Creole)"料理レストラン。南部ルイジアナを中心に生まれたこの料理は 18世紀の半ばに南フランスからの移民の人々が作り出したもの。"ケイジャン料理"はフランスの田舎料理で 様々な調味料やペッパー類を使用し アフリカン ルイジアナの影響を受けて生まれた。"クレオール料理"は 都会風で フランス スペイン アフリカ インドなどの影響を受け 辛味(スパイス)も少ない。店内はダイニングエリアの中央部に天井部から自然光を採りいれ ブース席も設けられシンプルなデザイン。このレストランは現在閉店している。
●ザ リッツ カフェ〈ロサンゼルス〉
現在閉店中 開店/1984年6月 客席数/162席 (レストラン150席 バー12席) 従業員数/80人

(Photo captions)
1 / The 150-seated dining area is simply designed so that natural light comes in the center.
2 / The restaurant in the South; serving dishes which mainly originated in Louisiana.
3 / The bar corner having a wide service space.

1/150席のダイニングは 中央部に自然光を取り入れシンプルなデザイン
2/アメリカ南部 ルイジアナを中心に生まれた料理を提供するレストラン
3/バーコーナー サービススペースを広く取っている

CAMPTON PLACE ⟨San Francisco⟩

A restaurant in "Campton Place Hotel" which stands near the Union Square, San Francisco. Inside the entrance in Italian Palladio style, one sees a spacious dining area across a glass partition whose swan is a symbol of the hotel. The interior is simply designed and the walls are decorated with apricot cloth frescos, thus creating an elegant and composed atmosphere. The chef is Mr. B. Ogden.

● CAMPTON PLACE (San Francisco)
Address/340 Stockton Street San Francisco, CA. 94108
Phone/415-781-5555
Opened/October 1983; Number of seats/88 (dining room 68, bar corner 20); Number of employees/35

サンフランシスコのユニオンスクエアに近い「キャンプトン プレイス ホテル」の中のレストラン。イタリアのパラディオ様式の入口を入ると このホテルのシンボルのスワンをデザインした ガラスのパーティション越しにゆったりしたダイニング席が見える。店内はシンプルなデザインで構成され 壁面にはアプリコットの布地を用いた壁画が飾られ エレガントで落ち着いた雰囲気のレストランである。シェフはB. Ogden氏。

●キャンプトン プレイス〈サンフランシスコ〉
Address/340 Stockton Street San Francisco, CA.94108 Phone/415-781-5555 開店/1983年10月 客席数/88席(ダイニングルーム68席 バーコーナー20席) 従業員数/35人

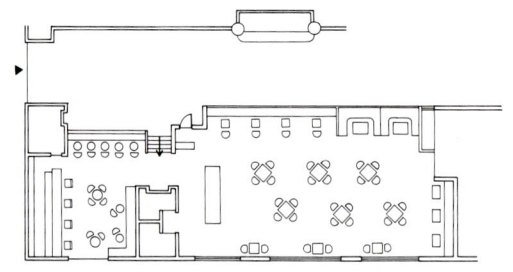

(Photo captions)
1 / The bar corner; used for various purposes — breakfast, tea time, cocktail party, etc.
2 / The entrance.
3 / The dining area, simply designed, has a dignified atmosphere.

1/バーコーナー 朝食 ティータイム カクテルなど多目的に利用される
2/エントランス
3/ダイニングエリア シンプルな中に格調の高さを感じさせる

WINDOWS ON THE WORLD ⟨New York⟩

"WINDOWS ON THE WORLD" is a unique restaurant complex using all of the 107th floor (4,050 m²) of "One World Trade Center" (about 400 m high) — northern half of the twin highrise World Trade Center Building which stands on the southern end of Manhattan, New York. It is composed of "The Grill" and the dining corner "The Statue of Liberty Lounge" on the south side, the bar, wine cellar and restaurant "The Cellar in the Sky" on the east side, the main dining "The Restaurant" on the north side, and 18 private rooms called private suites (used for dinner party, seminar, etc.) on the western window side. Designed by Mr. Warren Platner, the interior is characterized by such layout that the restaurant, bar and banquet areas are installed on the window side which has a splendid view, while the main dining space's kitchen, elevators, toilets and other equipment are concentrated in the central core part.

● WINDOWS ON THE WORLD (New York)
Address/107th floor New York Manhattan One World Trade Center Bldg., New York, N.Y.   Opened/1976

(Photo captions)
1 / The table in the buffet; foods are dished up ("The Restaurant").
2 / The wine rack beside the entrance (The Restaurant").
3 / Flowers are arranged by the entrance and simply designed lighting appliances are set on the ceiling ("The Restaurant").
4 / The dining area whose floor has different levels in consideration of privacy ("The Restaurant").

1/ビュッフェのテーブル 盛り付けた料理が置かれている(The Restaurant)
2/エントランス脇のワインラック(The Restaurant)
3/入口に花が置かれ 天井にはシンプルなデザインの照明がある
4/フロアレベルに段差をつけ プライバシーを配慮したダイニング(The Restaurant)

「ウィンドーズ オン ザ ワールド」は ニューヨークのマンハッタンの南端に建つ世界貿易センタービルのツインの超高層ビルのうち 北側の「ワン ワールド トレード センター」107階(高さ約400m)の全フロア(4,050m²)を使用したユニークなレストラン コンプレックスである。レストランの構成は 南側に「The Grill」とダイニングコーナーの「The Statue of Liberty Lounge」。東側にバー ワインセラーとレストラン「The Cellar in the Sky」と北側にかけてメインダイニングの「The Restaurant」がある。西側の窓側はすべてプライベート スイートと呼ばれる18の個室で 会食やセミナーなどに利用されている。設計はウォーレン プラトナー(Warren Platner)氏で レイアウトの特徴はレストランやバー 宴会場などが すべて眺めの良い窓側に面し メインのキッチン エレベーター トイレなどの施設が 中央コアの部分にまとめられていることである。

●ウィンドーズ オン ザ ワールド⟨ニューヨーク⟩
Address/107th floor New York Manhattan One World Trade Center bldg, New York, N.Y.   開店/1976年

DON ROTH'S RIVER PLAZA 〈Chicago〉

"DON ROTH'S RIVER PLAZA" is a restaurant managed by Mr. Don Roth who is said to be a "don" of American restaurant business. Here, typically American foods, such as prime rib, roast beef, broiled steak and fresh seafoods, are served. The restaurant is situated on the 1st and 2nd floors of an office building facing River Chicago. The 1st floor is used as the table seating area for both bar counter and lounge, while the 2nd floor is used as the main dining area. The interior uniformly uses earth color to give a wooden and earthy touch, and is simply finished without using tablecloth, thus producing a casual atmosphere. The lighting appliances using bamboos and window side screen are impressive, and through the screen one can enjoy a wonderful view of River Chicago and building highlights.

● DON ROTH'S RIVER PLAZA (Chicago)
Address/405 N. Wabash Chicago, Illinois
Opened/September 1980; Number of seats/174 (1st floor 54, 2nd floor 120)

(Photo captions)
1 / The main dining area under the bamboo-worked lighting appliances; through the screen one can see a wonderful street of Chicago.
2 / The dining area uses no tablecloth, producing a casual atmosphere.

アメリカのレストラン業界の"ドン"といわれるダン ロス(Don Roth)氏の経営するレストランで プライム リブやローストビーフ ブロイルド ステーキ フレッシュ シーフードといった典型的なアメリカ料理を提供している。「ダン ロス リバープラザ店」は シカゴ河に面したオフィスビルの1〜2階にある。1階はバーカウンターとラウンジを兼ねたテーブル席 2階はメインダイニングで構成されている。店内は木や土を感じさすアースカラーに統一され テーブルクロスもない気取らない雰囲気。竹を組み合わせた照明と窓際のブラインドが印象的でこれを透して見るシカゴ河とビルのハイライトはすばらしい。

● ダン ロス リバープラザ〈シカゴ〉
Address/405 N.Wabash Chicago,Illinois 開店/1980年9月 客席数/174席(1階 54席 2階 120席)

1/竹を組み合わせた照明があるメインダイニング ブラインドを透して見るシカゴのビル街はすばらしい
2/ダイニングはテーブルクロスもなく 気取らない雰囲気

MÖVENPIC ⟨New York⟩

A traditional European style restaurant whose main restaurant is situated in Zürich, Switzerland, "MÖVENPIC" in New York is operating on the 1st floor of "Sheraton City Square Hotel" which stands at a corner of Seventh Avenue at 51st Street. It is composed of the main dining area and bar lounge, together with an annex shop of croissant, and is also undertaking room services within the hotel. Favorably situated near an office street, shopping quarter, and also Broadway and Radio City. This restaurant is closed now.
● MÖVENPIC (New York)
Closed now; Opened/June 1981; Number of seats/213 (dining 175, bar 18, lounge 20); Number of employees/135

①

スイスのチューリッヒに本店を持つ伝統的なヨーロッパスタイルのこのレストランは 7番街と51丁目(Seventh Avenue at 51st Street)のコーナー「シェラトン シティ スクエア ホテル」の1階にある。クロワッサン ショップを併設しメインダイニングとバーラウンジで構成されホテル内のルームサービスも担当している。オフィス街 ショッピング街に合わせ ブロードウェイやラジオ シティに近い好立地である。このレストランは現在閉店している。
●モーベンピック ⟨ニューヨーク⟩
現在閉店中　開店/1981年6月　客席数/213席
(ダイニング175席　バー18席　ラウンジ20席)
従業員数/135人

②

(Photo captions)
1 / The table seating area employing the European atmosphere.
2 / The main dining area; with a terrace-like dining corner on the window side.
3 / The terrace room facing Seventh Avenue.

1/ヨーロッパの雰囲気を取り入れたテーブル席
2/メインダイニング　窓側はテラス風ダイニングコーナー
3/7番街(Seventh Avenue)に面したテラスルーム

BRAVO FONO ⟨Palo Alto, CA.⟩

A cafe operating in a shopping center near Stanford University in the south of San Francisco, "BRAVO FONO" mainly serves homemade sherbet, ice cream and desert, as well as Hungarian petit entrée, nine types of coffee, wine, beer and champagne. Accented with the marble floor, granite tabletops, etc., the interior is finished to give a bright, clean image.

● BRAVO FONO (Palo Alto, CA.)
Address/Stanford Shopping Center, 99 Palatine Court Palo Alto, CA.
Opened/December 1983; Number of seats/40; Number of employees/9

(Photo captions)
1 / The dining area; with an order counter in the center of the showcase.
2 / The terrace seating space under the bright skylight.

サンフランシスコの南 スタンフォード大学に近いショッピングセンターの中のカフェで 自家製のシャーベットやアイスクリーム デザート菓子をメインに ハンガリー料理のレシピのプチアントレと 9種類のコーヒーとワイン ビール シャンペンなどを提供している。大理石のフロア 御影石のテーブルトップなどをアクセントにした明るく清潔なイメージでまとめられている。

●ブラボー フォノ⟨カリフォルニア・パロ アルト⟩
Address/Stanford Shopping Center, 99 Palatine Court Palo Alto, CA. 開店/1983年12月 客席数/40席 従業員数/9人

ZUCCHINI'S ⟨Dallas, Texas⟩

Adopting "zucchini," which is very akin to cucumber, as its name, this restaurant comes with a "fresh market" in "Westin Hotel Galleria" in Dallas. Since it is adjacent to a shopping center, it is intended not merely for hotel guests but also for shoppers. The bright glazed interior walls are decorated with panels of vegetable & fruit corners at a supermarket, and there is actually a similar selling counter. Industrial lamps are used for lighting, accented with pink neons. The menu is mainly composed of soup, salads and sandwiches which are intended for freshness, health and nutrition.

● ZUCCHINI'S (Dallas, Texas)
Address/The Westin Hotel Galleria Dallas, 13340 Dallas Parkway at LBJ Freeway, Texas
Opened/January 1983; Number of seats/106

キュウリによく似たズッキーニを店名にし　フレッシュ　マーケットを持ち込んだカフェでダラスの「ウエスティン　ギャレリア　ホテル」にある。ショッピングセンターに隣接していることもあり　ホテルの利用客はもちろん買物客もターゲットにしている。ガラス張りの明るい店内の壁面には　スーパーマーケットの野菜　果物売り場のパネル写真が飾られ　同様の売り場を演出したカウンターを設け販売もしている。照明はインダストリアル　ランプを使用しピンクのネオンがアクセントをつけている。新鮮さと健康　栄養などを考えたスープ　サラダ　サンドイッチを中心としたメニュー構成である。

●ズッキーニ〈テキサス・ダラス〉
Address/The Westin Hotel Galleria Dallas, 13340 Dallas Parkway at LBJ Freeway, Texas
開店/1983年1月　客席数/106席

(Photo captions)
1 / The dining area whose wall is decorated with panels of selling corners at a supermarket.
2 / The service station and market counter viewed from the cashier's desk before the selling corner.

1/ダイニングエリア　スーパーマーケットの売り場のパネル写真が飾られている
2/物販コーナーのキャッシャーより　サービス　ステーションとマーケット　カウンターをみる

THE PINK PEAR ⟨Atlanta, Georgia⟩

Sandy Spring in the suburbs of Atlanta is a town where many "professionals." Managed by Mr. & Mrs. Ehrhardt, "PINK PEAR" provides them with catering service and carry-out. It satisfies all customer needs such as catering parties and renting properties; at the cafe's sales corner, party dishes and drinks are sold. On the cafe terrace facing the garden, lunch and after tea are offered.
● THE PINK PEAR (Atlanta, Georgia)
Address/369 Sandy Spring Circle Atlanta, Georgia 30328
Phone/404-256-5589
Opened/December 1983; Number of seats/40; Number of employees/9

アトランタ郊外のサンディ スプリングの町はプロフェッショナルと呼ばれる専門職の人たちが多く住むところで これらの人たちを対象にケータリング サービスとキャリィアウトを手掛けているのが エアハート(Ehrhardt)夫妻の「ザ ピンク ペアー」である。この店では出張料理とパーティの演出から小道具のレンタルまで いっさいのニーズに応えるとともに カフェの売店では 惣菜やパーティ料理 飲物などを販売している。そして庭に面したカフェテラスでは ランチとアフターティを提供している。
●ザ ピンク ペアー ⟨ジョージア・アトランタ⟩
Address/369 Sandy Spring Circle Atlanta, Georgia 30328　Phone/404-256-5589　開店/1983年12月　客席数/40席　従業員数/9人

(Photo captions)
1 / The interior utilizes "pink" as the theme color. The shop offers dishes and drinks necessary for party/picnic.
2 / A van used for catering service.

1/テーマカラーのピンクを活かした店内 パーティ ピクニック用の料理 飲物が揃っている
2/ケータリング サービスに使用されるバン

LANGAN'S BRASSERIE ⟨Los Angeles⟩

Headquartered in London, "LANGAN'S BRASSERIE" opened its branch shop in a shopping center in Century City. Featuring an all-time operation, it starts with breakfast menu, followed by lunch menu, small menu and dinner menu. The interior (11,000 sq. feet), having an atmosphere of Bahama, is decorated with watercolor and oil paintings, and provided with a cherry wood bar counter longer than 20 m, a seafood bar serving fresh oyster, shrimps, crab, etc.
● LANGAN'S BRASSERIE (Los Angeles)
Address/10250 Santa Monica Boulevard Los Angeles, CA. 90067
Phone/213-785-0961
Opened/June 1988; Number of seats/310 (dining area 180, bar area 130); Number of employees/120

ロンドンに本店を持つ「ランガンズ ブラッスリー」がセンチュリー シティ（Century City）のショッピングセンター内に出店した。オールタイムの営業で　朝食メニューにはじまり　ランチメニュー　スモールメニュー　ディナーメニューで構成されている。バハマの雰囲気の11,000平方フィートの店内には　水彩画や油絵が飾られ　20m以上もあるチェリーウッドのバーカウンターと新鮮なカキやシュリンプ　カニなどをサービスするシーフードバーなどが設けられている。
●ランガンズ ブラッセリー〈ロサンゼルス〉
Address/10250 Santa Monica Boulevard Los Angeles, CA.90067　Phone/213-785-0961　開店/1988年6月　客席数/310席（ダイニングエリア180席　バーエリア130席）　従業員数/120人

(Photo captions)
1 / The facade surrounded with palm trees.
2 / The entrance area viewed from an inner part of the spacious dining area.
3 / The dining area; with the bar counter longer than 20 m.

1/パームツリーに囲まれたファサード
2/広いダイニングエリアの奥からエントランス方向をみる
3/ダイニングエリア　バーカウンターは20m以上の長さがある

THE VELVET TURTLE 〈City of Industry, CA.〉

A restaurant situated in City of Industry, about 35 km east of Los Angeles, where airplane, electronics, iron & steel and other factories, offices, shopping centers and residences are increasing. Mainly serving steak and seafoods, "THE VELVET TURTLE" is designed in the Tudor style.
● THE VELVET TURTLE
 (City of Industry, CA.)
Address/17555 Castleton City of Industry, CA. 91745
Number of seats/295 (restaurant 220, bar 75); Number of employees/110

ロサンゼルスの東　約35kmのシティ オブ インダストリー（City of Industry）と呼ばれる航空機や電子工学　鉄鋼関係の工場やオフィス　ショッピングセンター　住宅などが増加しているそんな地域に立地しているレストラン。ステーキとシーフードがメインで　イギリスのチューダー調のデザインでまとめられている。
●ザ ベルベット タートル〈カリフォルニア・シティ オブ インダストリー〉
Address/17555 Castleton City of Industry, CA. 91745　客席数/295席（レストラン220席　バー75席）　従業員数/110人

(Photo captions)
1 / The facade akin to an English private house.
2 / The bar area adopting a top light.
3 / The waiting area; finished like an English drawing room decorated with a collection of paintings.
4 / The dining room accented with white arched pillars.

1/イギリスの民家風のファサード
2/トップライトを取り入れたバーエリア
3/ウェイティングエリア　応接間風で絵画のコレクションが飾られている
4/白いアーチ状の柱が配されたダイニングルーム

RUSTY SCUPPER ⟨San Francisco⟩

Just as the catchphrase "RUSTY SCUPPER" is a restaurant running between important ports from San Francisco to Boston" implies, "RUSTY SCUPPER" is a dinner type restaurant chain developing across the United States. "Scupper" means a hole made in the ship side so that water flows down from the deck, and "Rusty Scupper" means a tugboat which sails against the raging storm in San Francisco Bay. Designed by Ed Steevens, an architect in Massachusetts, the interior adopted an "organic architecture" which is functional but stresses nature.

● RUSTY SCUPPER (San Francisco)
Address/1800 Montgomery San Francisco, CA.
Opened/June 1978;   Number of seats/375 (restaurant 210, bar 165);   Number of employees/103

"「ラスティ スカッパー」は サンフランシスコからボストンまでの重要な港の間を運行しているレストランです" と謳っているように 全米にまたがってチェーン展開しているディナータイプのレストランである。"スカッパー" とは水がデッキから流れるように船の横腹にある穴のことで 店名の「ラスティ スカッパー」はサンフランシスコ湾に荒れくるう嵐に逆航するタグボートのことを意味するという。設計はマサチューセッツの建築家Ed Steevens氏で オーガニック アーキテクチュアと呼ばれ 機能的であり なお自然を強調することを意図したデザインになっている。

●ラスティ スカッパー〈サンフランシスコ〉
Address/1800 Montgomery San Francisco, CA.
開店/1978年6月　客席数/375席(レストラン210席　バー165席)　従業員数/103人

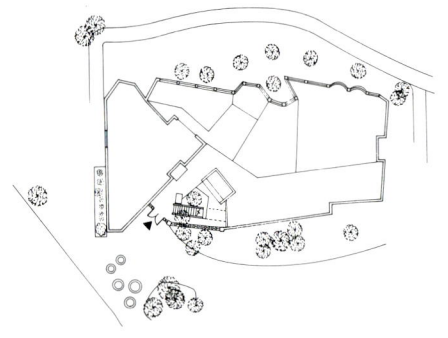

(Photo captions)
1 / The unique facade of the restaurant.
2 / The dining room; incorporating the ceiling ducts as part of the interior, the interior features wood colors to give a warm and composed atmosphere.
3 / The bar counter finished with Italian tiles.

1/ユニークなレストランのファサード
2/ダイニングルーム　天井のダクトをインテリアに取り入れ色彩も木を意識した温かい落ち着きのあるものにしている
3/イタリアンタイルを貼ったバーカウンター

COOK BOOK ⟨El Toro, CA.⟩

Mainly developing its chain in California, "COOK BOOK" is a restaurant offering 168 types of omelets. The building is finished so that it looks like a traditional Portuguese house whose interior utilizes wood to create a bright, homely atmosphere. The restaurant is surrounded with retired people's facilities and houses, and close to Laguna Beach by car. Thus, since the area is good for health and has a fine climate, residents are increasing.
● COOK BOOK (El Toro, CA.)
Address/El Toro, CA.
Opened/June 1982;   Number of seats/229;
Number of employees/35

(Photo captions)
1 / The buffet counter of the restaurant accented with street lamps so that the interior looks like a restaurant with a sidewalk.
2 / The dining room; green elements are employed abundantly under the ceiling top light.
3 / The booth seating area having a homely atmosphere.

カリフォルニアを中心にチェーン展開しているこのレストランは 168種のオムレツが売りもの。建物はポルトガルの民家風の造りで 店内は木を活かした明るい家庭的な雰囲気を演出している。レストランの周辺は リタイアした人たちの施設や住宅 車で少し走ればラグナビーチにも近く 健康や気候の良さで移り住む人たちが増えている場所である。
● クックブック ⟨カリフォルニア・エルトロ⟩
Address/El Toro, CA.　開店/1982年6月　客席数/229席　従業員数/35人

1/街灯を配しサイドウォークの店を演出したレストランのビュッフェカウンター
2/ダイニングルーム　天井にトップライトを設け　グリーンを多く取り入れている
3/家庭的な雰囲気のブース席

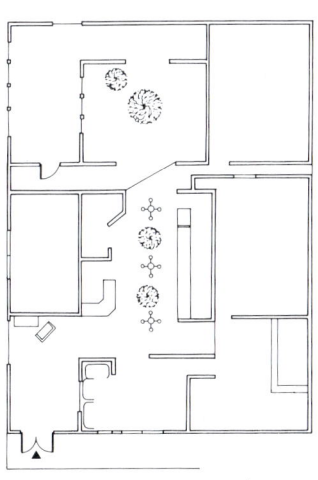

FORTY CARROTS ⟨Tarrance, CA.⟩

As might be imagined from the shop name, "FORTY CARROTS" features a unique menu composed of healthy drinks using fresh vegetables and fruits, and items selected from Italian, Mexican and American foods. The interior is designed to create a warm and natural atmosphere by heavily using the carrot color, green and white. Napkins in glass set on the table image carrots, which also serve as an eye-catcher. The modern and simple interior design stresses brightness, cleanliness and health. The restaurant is closed now.

● FORTY CARROTS (Tarrance, CA.)
Closed now;   Opened/September 1980;
Number of seats/172;   Number of employees/80

「Forty Carrots」の店名からも想像されるように 新鮮な野菜や果物を食材にしたヘルシードリンクやイタリア メキシコ アメリカ料理などから独自のメニュースタイルを造り出している。インテリアは温かさや自然を強調し 人参の色と緑や白などを多く使用している。テーブルセッティングされたグラスの中のナプキンは人参をイメージしたものであり アイキャッチにもなっている。モダンでシンプルなデザインであるが 明るさや清潔さを強調し 健康をアッピールしている。このレストランは現在閉店されている。

●フォーティキャロッツ〈カリフォルニア・トーランス〉
現在閉店中　開店/1980年9月　客席数/172席
従業員数/80人

(Photo captions)
1 / The interior presentation which is said to have a New York sense; carrot-shaped napkins set on the table serve as an eye-catcher.
2 / The bright, terrace-like dining area; the mirror on the inner wall gives an expansive image.
3 / The carrot-colored bar corner.

1/ニューヨーク感覚といわれる演出 テーブルセッティングされた人参をイメージしたナプキンがアイキャッチャーになっている
2/明るいテラス風のダイニングルエリア 奥の壁面のミラーが広がりをあたえている
3/人参の色のバーコーナー

RAINBOW PIER FISH MARKET 〈Long Beach, CA.〉

A seafood restaurant in "Shoreline Village" on Long Beach which is composed of a shopping, dining and entertainment attraction facilities, aimed to "reproduce a coast a century ago." It is situated at a corner of a harbor where the deluxe liner Queen Mary anchors, and there also is a yacht marina nearby. Inside, there is a large water tank into which fish/shellfish caught in the nearby sea are brought, and these fish/shellfish are sold while they are alive or cooked for guests.

● RAINBOW PIER FISH MARKET (Long Beach, CA.)
Address/423 Shoreline Village Drive Long Beach, CA. 90802
Opened/October 1983; Number of seats/100; Number of employees/25〜30

"一世紀前の海岸の再現"をテーマにしたロングビーチのショッピングとダイニング エンターテイメント アトラクション施設で構成される「ショアライン ヴィレッジ (Shoreline Village)」にあるシーフードレストラン。豪華客船クイーン メリー号が停泊するハーバーの一画に位置し 周囲にはヨットのマリーナもある。店内には大きな水槽が置かれ 近海で漁れた魚介類が運び込まれる。活きたまま小売りされ 料理もして食べさせてくれる。

●レインボー ピア フィシュ マーケット〈カリフォルニア・ロングビーチ〉
Address/423 Shoreline Village Drive Long Beach, CA.90802 開店/1983年10月 客席数/100席 従業員数/25〜30人

(Photo captions)
1 / The facade expressing a light blue beach house.
2 / The eat in seating area whose floor is covered with sand to give a seaside image and casual atmosphere.
3 / The bar corner.
4 / The fresh fish/shellfish selling corner.

1/ライトブルーの海の家を表現したファサード
2/フロアに砂をまき海岸をイメージし カジュアルに演出されたイートイン席
3/バーコーナーをみる
4/新鮮な魚介類の販売コーナー

VICTORIA STATION 〈Universal City, CA.〉

Situated within the site of Universal Studio, "VICTORIA STATION" may be said to be a complete compilation of the chain which is developing rapidly by pursuing "railway" as its theme. The domed facade gives such an impression that one feels as if Victoria Station in London has just appeared before oneself. The interior is decorated with passenger carriages, a large four-sided clock, a schedule panel showing train departures, etc. which were actually used in England — amusing not merely to railway-manias but also ordinary guests.

● VICTORIA STATION
 (Universal City, CA.)
Address/100 Universal City Plaza Universal City, CA.
Opened/May 1977;　　Number of seats/600

鉄道をテーマに展開している「ビクトリア ステーション」の集大成ともいえるこの店は　アメリカの代表的な映画スタジオの一つ　ユニバーサル スタジオの敷地内にある。円形のドームのあるファサードは　ロンドンのビクトリア駅がそこに出現したような錯覚を与えるスケールの大きさだ。店内にはイギリスで実際に使われていた客車や　ビクトリア駅の4面の大時計　発着を示すスケジュール板などマニアでなくても楽しめる演出である。

●ビクトリアステーション〈カリフォルニア・ユニバーサルシティ〉
Address/100 Universal City Plaza Universal City, CA．　開店/1977年5月　客席数/600席

(Photo captions)
1 / The octagonal entrance hall and bar corner under the dome; the clock schedule panel was actually used.
2 / The facade copying Victoria Station in London.
3 / The dining corner imaging a station shed.
4 / The guest seating area on the platform; passenger carriages on both sides serve a dining rooms.

1/ドーム下の8角形のエントランスホールとバーコーナー　時計やスケジュールパネルは実際に使用されていたもの
2/ロンドンのビクトリア駅を模したファサード
3/駅の格納庫をイメージしたダイニングコーナー
4/プラットホームにある客席　両側の客車はダイニングルーム

D.B. KAPLAN'S ⟨Chicago⟩

A restaurant serving 153 types of sandwich, 18 types of flavor and 23 items of ice cream. The interior uses four primary colors — red, yellow, green and blue — thereby creating a garden-like atmosphere. Located on the 7th floor of the shopping center "Water Tower Place" which faces Michigan Avenue, a central shopping quarter in Chicago, "D.B. KAPLAN'S" is visited by customers all day long.

● D.B. KAPLAN'S (Chicago)
Address/Water Tower Place 7th floor, 845 North Michigan Avenue Chicago, Illinois 60611
Opened/1977; Number of seats/260; Number of employees/100

153種類のサンドイッチと18種類のフレーバー 23アイテムのアイスクリームを揃えたレストラン。店内には赤 黄 緑 青の原色が多く使われ ガーデン風の雰囲気を持たせている。シカゴのショッピングの中心地のミシガン アベニューに面した ショッピングセンター「ウォーター タワー プレイス(Water Tower Place)」の7階にあるこの店は ランチタイムを中心に終日利用客が行列している

●ディ ビー カプランズ ⟨シカゴ⟩
Address/Water Tower Place 7th floor, 845 North Michigan Avenue Chicago, Illinois 60611 開店/1977年 客席数/260席 従業員数/100人

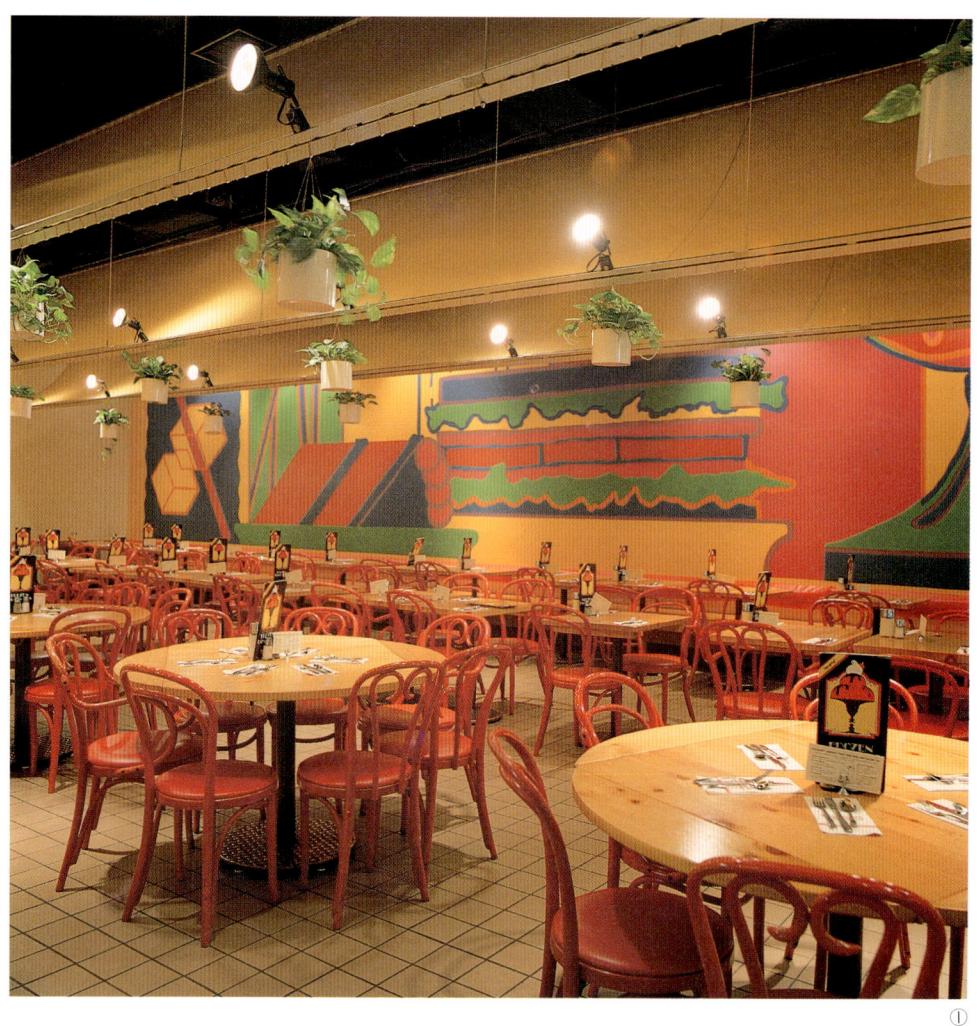

(Photo captions)
1 / The dining area whose wall is colorfully finished.
2 / The bar counter; drinks ranging from hard liquor to beer and wine are served.
3 / The dining area taking up a sandwich as its wall decor theme; the ceiling is tented to create a garden-like atmosphere.

1/カラフルな壁画で構成されたダイニングエリア
2/バーカウンター ハードリカーからビールやワインなどのドリンクスがサービスされる
3/サンドイッチをテーマにした作品があるダイニング 天井にはテントが張られ ガーデン風の雰囲気を演出している

RED ROBIN ⟨Los Alamitos, CA.⟩

A restaurant chain headquartered in Seattle, "RED ROBIN" is developing its operations with a menu mainly composed of gourmet burgers and unique cocktail drinks. The facade of "RED ROBIN" at Los Alamitos, coupled with a large signboard, stands out with red stripes against the white base. A sunroom is installed facing the front yard so that the dining room looks spacious—the bar area and service station, among others, are spaciously installed. Intended to become a new-type casual restaurant for family guests, young professionals, etc.

● RED ROBIN (Los Alamitos, CA.)
Address/4232 Katella Avenue Los Alamitos, CA. 90270
Phone/213-594-4601
Opened/September 1985; Number of seats/255; Number of employees/107

(Photo captions)
1 / The entrance and bar lounge.
2 / The casual dining area.
3 / The bright dining room in sunroom style.

シアトルに本社を置き グルメバーガーとユニークなカクテルドリンクスを主なメニューとして店舗展開しているレストラン。この「ロス アラミトス店」のファサードは 白を基調に赤いストライプでまとめ 大きなサインボードとともにかなり目立つものになっている。フロントヤードに面してサンルームを設け ダイニングエリアに広がりを持たせ 特にバーエリアやサービス ステーションなどにも広いスペースを取っている。ファミリー客や若いプロフェッショナルをターゲットにした新しいタイプのカジュアルレストランを目指している。

●レッド ロビン〈カリフォルニア・ロス アラミトス〉
Address/4232 Katella Avenue Los Alamitos, CA. 90270 Phone/213-594-4601 開店/1985年9月 客席数/255席 従業員数/107人

1/エントランスとバーラウンジ
2/カジュアルにまとめられたダイニングエリア
3/明るいサンルーム造りのダイニングルーム

①

②

③

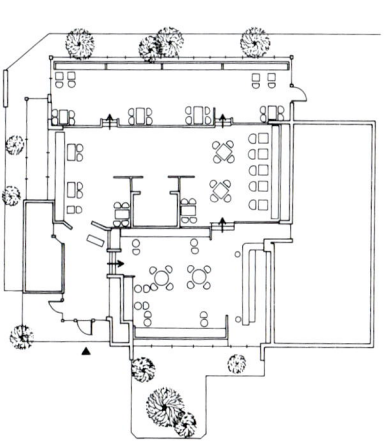

ORGAN GRINDER ⟨Denver, Colorado⟩

A pizza restaurant in which a huge pipe harmonium is installed and guests can enjoy dynamic performance while eating. It is said that, in the 1920s when silent films were at their height, a theater pipe harmonium was played to the accompaniment of film. It is intended to create such a theatrical atmosphere. On the pillars and ceiling about 12,000 small electric bulbs are lined and their luminous intensity is changed according to stress of the pipe harmonium sound. Thus, "ORGAN GRINDER" is a theater-style restaurant.

● ORGAN GRINDER (Denver, Colorado)
Address/2370 W. Alemeda Boulevard Denver, Colorado 80223
Opened/February 1979;   Number of seats/564;   Number of employees/135

巨大なパイプオルガンを店内に備え 食事をしながらダイナミックな演奏が楽しめるピザレストラン。1920年代 無声映画全盛の頃 映画の伴奏のためにシアター パイプオルガンが使用されたという そんな劇場の雰囲気がテーマになっている。店内の柱や天井には12,000個もの小さな電球が連なり オルガンの音の強弱にあわせて光量が変化する演出がなされたシアター形式のレストランである。

●オーガングラインダー〈コロラド・デンバー〉
Address/2370 W. Alemeda Boulevard Denver, Colorado 80223 開店/1979年2月 客席数/564席 従業員数/135人

(Photo captions)
1 / The dining area; the luminous intensity of 12,000 bulbs changes with stress of the pipe harmonium sound.
2 / The facade and large signboard remind us of a theater.

1/ダイニングエリア パイプオルガンの音の強弱で12,000個の電球の光量が変化する
2/劇場を思わせるファサードと大きなサインボード

①
②

HAMLET GARDENS ⟨Los Angeles⟩

The building used for "HAMLET GARDENS" was originally constructed in 1931 in Westwood, a student town where UCLA is situated. It was redecorated to open the restaurant. The restaurant has 7,000 sq. ft. of space which is composed of four dining rooms. The upper part of the main dining room in the center (called the "courtyard") forms a stairwell 30 feet high under the glass dome ceiling. The interior is rich with greenery and abundantly uses time-honored tiles, European natural stone and pavement materials, thus reminding us of a French château or countryside.

● HAMLET GARDENS (Los Angeles)
Address/1139 Glendon of Lindbrook Westwood Los Angeles, CA. 90024
Phone/213-824-1818
Opened/January 1986;   Number of seats/160;   Number of employees/120

UCLAがある学生の街・ウエストウッドの1931年に建てられた古い建物を改装しオープンした「ハムレット ガーデンズ」。7,000平方フィートのスペースを持つこの店は　4つのダイニングルームで構成されている。中央のコートヤードと呼ぶメインダイニングの上部は30フィートの高さの吹き抜けで　天井部はガラスのドームになっている。店内には　グリーンが多く取り入れられ　年代物のタイルやヨーロッパの自然石舗装材をふんだんに使用したフランスのシャトーや田舎を思わせる造りになっている。

●ハムレット ガーデンズ〈ロサンゼルス〉
Address/1139 Glendon of Londbrook Westwood Los Angeles, CA. 90024   Phone/213-824-1818
開店/1986年1月　客席数/160席　従業員数/120人

(Photo captions)
1 / The dining area which utilizes the brick ground.
2 / The dining room accented with marble tables; gives a château's atmosphere.
3 / The main dining room whose upper part forms a stairwell under the glass dome ceiling.
4 / The facade; the main dining area lies under the central dome.

1/煉瓦地を活かしたダイニングエリア
2/大理石のテーブルを配したダイニングルーム　シャトーを思わせる雰囲気
3/メインダイニング　上部は吹き抜けになっており　天井はガラスのドームになっている
4/ファサード　中央ドームの下がメインダイニングになっている

①

②

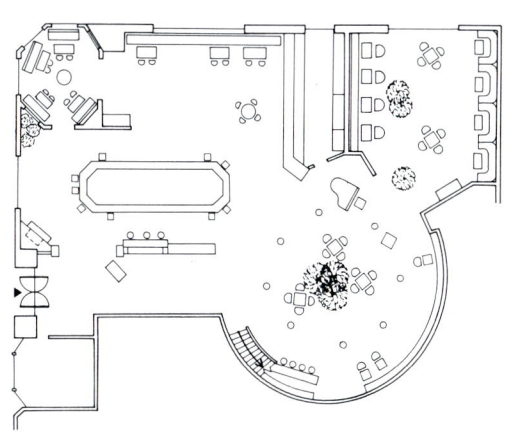

ファストフード & カフェテリアレストラン

サラダ プラス〈カリフォルニア・アップランド〉 218
ザ カフェ アット ビトウィーン ザ ブレッド〈ニューヨーク〉 220
101 シンクス トゥー イート〈ニューヨーク〉 221
フレイキィ ジェイクス〈カリフォルニア・ウエスト ロサンゼルス〉 222
ウェルドンズ〈カリフォルニア・コスタ メサ〉 224
マクドナルド〈シカゴ〉 226
ジ オーゲーム ピザ コラル〈カリフォルニア・モントクレア〉 228
スバーロ〈ニューヨーク〉 229
ピクニック フード コート〈コロラド・デンバー〉 230
ザ マーケット〈ニューヨーク〉 232
インターナショナル フード ワークス〈ジョージア・アトランタ〉 234
フルトン マーケット〈ニューヨーク〉 236

Fast food & Cafeteria restaurants

SALADS PLUS ⟨Upland, CA.⟩ 218
THE CAFE AT BETWEEN THE BREAD ⟨New York⟩ 220
101 THINGS TO EAT ⟨New York⟩ 221
FLAKEY JAKE'S ⟨West Los Angeles, CA.⟩ 222
WELDON'S ⟨Costa Mesa, CA.⟩ 224
McDONALD'S ⟨Chicago⟩ 226
THE O-GAME PIZZA CORRAL ⟨Montclair, CA.⟩ 228
SBARRO ⟨New York⟩ 229
PICNIC FOOD COURT ⟨Denver, CO.⟩ 230
THE MARKET ⟨New York⟩ 232
INTERNATIONAL FOOD WORKS ⟨Atlanta, Georgia⟩ 234
FULTON MARKET ⟨New York⟩ 236

SALADS PLUS 〈Upland, CA.〉

A restaurant chain whose salad bar offers more than 50 types of salad, "SALADAS PLUS" chain is mainly developing in California. Upland, where this restaurant is situated, is in the hills to the northwest of Los Angeles. This area is composed of light industrial facilities, offices, residences, etc. The interior is in a bright cafeteria style, and on the walls shop name logos and vegetable illustrations are painted, thus giving a bold image.
● SALADAS PLUS (Upland, CA.)
Address/577 North Mountain Upland, CA.
Opened/August 1980; Number of seats/105 (restaurant 81, terrace 24); Number of employees/24

50種以上の材料を揃えたサラダバーが売りもののレストランで カリフォルニアを中心にチェーン展開している。この店のあるアップランド(Upland)は ロサンゼルスの北西部に位置する丘陵地帯で 軽工業やオフィス 住宅地などで構成される場所。店内はカフェテリア スタイルで明るく 壁面には店名のロゴや野菜のイラストが描かれ 大胆なイメージをあたえている。
●サラダ プラス〈カリフォルニア・アップランド〉
Address/577 North Mountain Upland, CA. 開店/1980年8月　客席数/105席(レストラン81席 テラス席24席)　従業員数/24人

①

(Photo captions)
1 / The dining area viewed from the entrance.
2 / The deep interior is bright by introducing natural light; the shop name logo is painted on the wall.
3 / The vegetable illustrations on the wall give a bold image.

1/入口からダイニングエリアをみる
2/自然光を取り入れ明るく奥行きのある店内 壁面には店名のロゴが描かれている
3/壁面の野菜のイラストが大胆なイメージをあたえる

②

THE CAFE AT BETWEEN THE BREAD 〈New York〉

Having a unique name, "THE CAFE AT BETWEEN THE BREAD" mainly serves salads and sandwiches. With white and sand colors as the basic tone, the interior is partly accented with wine color on the pillars and walls, thus forming a bright, contemporary composition. The restaurant is closed now.
● THE CAFE AT BETWEEN THE BREAD (New York)
Closed now; Opened/June 1983; Number of seats/162 (table 122, garden 40); Number of employees/40

(Photo caption)
The dining area featuring a contemporary design; the bar corner at the back.

"パンにはさまれたカフェ"というユニークな店名の サラダとサンドイッチがメインのレストラン。店内は 白やサンドカラーを基調に柱や壁面の一部にはワインカラーをアクセントとして使用し 明るいコンテンポラリーな構成になっている。このレストランは現在閉店されている。
● ザ カフェ アット ビトゥイーン ザ ブレッド 〈ニューヨーク〉
現在閉店中 開店/1983年6月 客席数/162席 (テーブル席122席 ガーデン40席) 従業員数/40人

コンテンポラリーなデザインのダイニングエリア 奥はバーコーナー

101 THINGS TO EAT ⟨New York⟩

A cafeteria restaurant situated in "101 Park Building" on the south side of Grand Central Station in New York, "101 THINGS TO EAT" offers a menu mainly composed of sandwiches, cold plates, hot entrée and special items which change daily. With a creamy counter and floor tiles, the interior gives a bright image. Neoned stations are used to separately display grills, hot delis, delis, specialities, ice cream, drinks, etc. In sharp contrast to the cafeteria, the dining area features dim lighting to create a dinner house atmosphere.

● 101 THINGS TO EAT (New York)
Address/101 Park Avenue New York, N.Y. 10178
Opened/December 1982; Number of seats/470

ニューヨークのグランド セントラル駅の南側101パークビルにあるカフェテリア レストラン。サンドイッチ類とコールド プレート ホットアントレと日替わりスペシャルなどのメニュー構成。クリーム色のカウンターやフロアのタイルが明るく 清潔なイメージを与え グリルやホットデリ デリ スペシャリティーズ アイスクリーム ドリンクスなどに分けられている。ステーションの上部にはネオンが配してある。ダイニングエリアは カフェテリアとは対象的に照明をおさえディナーハウスの雰囲気を演出している。
●101 シングス トゥー イート⟨ニューヨーク⟩
Address/101 Park Avenue New York, N.Y. 10178 開店/1982年12月 客席数/470席

(Photo captions)
1 / The cafeteria; with the neoned stations which give a clean image.
2 / The dining area; presenting a dinner house atmosphere with dim lighting.

1/カフェテリア 清潔感をあたえるステーションにはネオンが配されている
2/ダイニングエリア 照明をおさえディナーハウスの雰囲気を演出

FLAKEY JAKE'S 〈West Los Angeles, CA.〉

Headquartered in Dallas, "FLAKEY JAKE'S" is developing a chain of hamburger and bakery shops in the main, intended for young adults and family guests. The interior is decorated with neon signs, movie posters of good old days, etc., thus giving a casual atmosphere.

● FLAKEY JAKE'S (West Los Angeles, CA.)
Address/2347 Sepulveda West Los Angeles, CA. 90025
Phone/206-644-9467
Opened/1983; Number of seats/266 (dining 242—including no-smoking seats 54, bar 26)

(Photo captions)
1 / The dining area is decorated with neons and movie posters, thus giving a casual atmosphere.
2 / The dining area; with the central slope for wheelchair users which also serves as a service aisle.
3 / The order counter.

1/ネオンや映画のポスターが飾られたカジュアルな雰囲気のダイニング
2/ダイニングエリア 中央のスロープは車椅子の利用を配慮したもので サービス通路にもなっている
3/オーダーカウンター

ダラスに本部を置き 店舗展開しているハンバーガーとベーカリーを中心としたファストフードレストランで ヤングアダルトやファミリー客をターゲットにしている。店内はネオンや懐かしい映画のポスターなどが飾られ カジュアルな雰囲気のレストランである。

●フレイキィ ジェイクス〈カリフォルニア・ウエスト ロサンゼルス〉
Address/2347 Sepulveda West Los Angeles, CA. 90025 Phone/206-644-9467 開店/1983年 客席数/268席(ダイニング242席 内54席は禁煙席 バー26席)

①

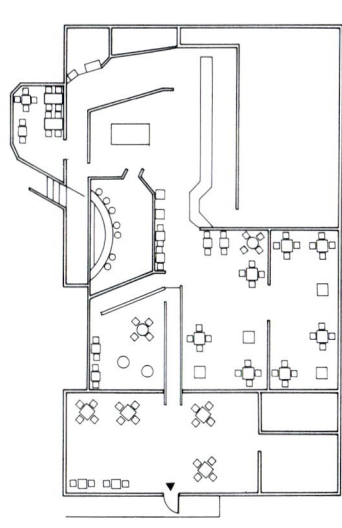

WELDON'S 〈Costa Mesa, CA.〉

Serving hot dogs, hamburgers, chicken sandwiches, Cajun stuff, Mexican stuffed potatoes, etc., "WELDON'S" is a restaurant mainly intended for adults aged 25 to 40. The interior is accented with a unique character named "Weldon" around which a colorful world is presented. On the upper wall of the dining area imaginary scenes are drawn. From "Weldon World Station" located just in front of the central order counter, a miniature train departs and continues to run in the restaurant. Thus, "WELDON'S" introduces entertainment and dreams into the interior presentation.
● WELDON'S (Costa Mesa, CA.)
Address/250 S. Bristol Street Costa Mesa, CA. 92626
Opened/December 1985;   Number of seats/80;   Number of employees/40

ホットドック ハンバーガー チキンサンドなどにケイジャン料理(Cajun Stuff)やメキシコポテト料理を提供している「ウェルドンズ」は25～40歳位までのアダルトな層を対象としたレストラン。店内には"ウェルドン"というユニークなキャラクターを作り カラフルな世界を展開している。ダイニングエリアの上部壁面には 想像上の風景が描かれ 中央オーダー カウンターの正面に位置する"ウェルドン ワールド駅"から発車したミニチュアの汽車が 店内をぐるりと走り続けるなど エンターテイメントと夢を持ち込んだ演出をしている。
●ウェルドンズ〈カリフォルニア・コスタ メサ〉
Address/250 S.Bristol Street Costa Mesa, CA. 92626 開店/1985年12月 客席数/80席 従業員数/40人

(Photo captions)
1 / The facade of "WELDON'S" imaging a palace.
2 / The counter area featuring clean and amusing presentation; seen above is the painted "Weldon's Station."
3・4 / The colorful dining area; a miniature train runs along the paintings drawn on the upper wall of the central order counter.

1/宮殿をイメージした「ウェルドン」のファサード
2/清潔で楽しさを演出したカウンター 上部に"ウェルドン ワールド"駅の絵がみえる
3・4/カラフルなダイニングエリア 中央オーダーカウンターの上部壁面に描かれた絵の中をミニチュアの汽車が走る

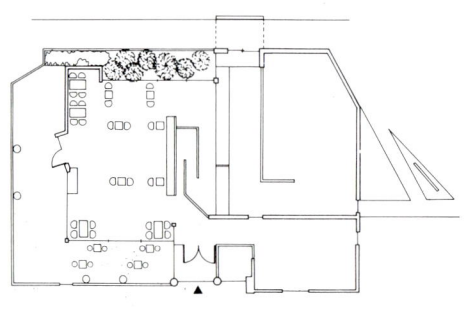

McDONALD'S ⟨Chicago⟩

"McDONALD'S" at River North takes up the 1950s and 1960s as its design themes by using two corners. The "'50s Corner" is decorated with Colbet's open car made in 1959, Phillip 66's gasoline pump, etc., and the '50s hit songs are aired from Wurlitzer's jukebox. The "'60s Corner" features encased life-size dolls of Beatles members around which counter and table seating areas are installed, and the '60s hit songs are aired. The walls are decorated with posters, toys, automobile parts, record jackets, etc.

● McDONALD'S (Chicago)
Address/600 North Clark Street Chicago, Illinois 60610
Phone/312-664-7940
Opened/1986; Number of seats/445 (restaurant 345, banquet 100)

(Photo captions)
1 / The '60s Corner is popular with life-size dolls of Beatles, and posters of Presley, etc. displayed on the wall.
2・4 / The '50s Corner is finished with black & grey as the basic tone; the wall is decorated with various types of collection.
3 / The order counter features a metallic finish where employees in the '50s uniform are serving.

「マクドナルド リバーノース店」は 1950年と'60年代をデザインのテーマにしている。'50年代をテーマにしたコーナーは 1959年製のコルベットのオープンカーやフィリップ66のガソリンポンプを飾り ワーリッツァー製のジュークボックスからは '50年代のヒットソングを流している。'60年代のコーナーには 等身大のビートルズの人形がケースの中に飾られ その周りにカウンター席やテーブル席があり '60年代のヒット曲が流れている。壁面には当時のポスターやおもちゃ 車のパーツ レコードジャケットなどが飾られている。

● マクドナルド ⟨シカゴ⟩
Address/600 North Clark Street Chicago, Illinois 60610　Phone/312-664-7940　開店/1986年　客席数/445席（レストラン345席 バンケット100席）

1/'60年代のコーナーはビートルズの等身大の人形やプレスリーのポスターがディスプレイされ人気がある
2・4/'50年代のコーナーは黒とグレーが基本カラー 壁面にはコレクションがいろいろ飾られている
3/オーダーカウンター メタリックな素材で造られ '50年代のユニフォームの従業員がサービスしている

①

②

③

THE O-GAME PIZZA CORRAL 〈Montclair CA.〉

Adjacent to a shopping center, this pizza restaurant is operating in an amusement center which combines eating & drinking and amusement facilities. By incorporating a "cattle pen" image into the decor, the interior design takes up the West in the days of pioneers as its theme. The interior utilizes wood grain finish to create an atmosphere like a cattle pen; from the high ceiling with a sky light, a wagon is suspended. Since a game center is annexed, guests can enjoy TV game while waiting for their pizzas being toasted.

● THE O-GAME PIZZA CORRAL
(Montclair CA.)
Address/9365 Monte Vista Avenue Montclair, CA. 91763
Opened/July 1981;   Number of seats/150;
Number of employees/35

このピザレストランは ショッピングセンターに隣接し 飲食と娯楽施設を集合したアミューズメントセンターの中にある。家畜の囲いをデコアに取り入れ 開拓時代の西部をデザインのテーマにしている。木目を活かした店内は家畜小屋の雰囲気で 高い天窓のある天井からはワゴンが吊り下げられている。ゲーム場を併設しており ピザが焼き上がるまでテレビゲームを楽しむことができる。

●ジ オーゲーム ピザ コラル〈カリフォルニア・モントクレア〉
Address/9365 Monte Vista Avenue Montclair, CA. 91763　開店/1981年7月　客席数/150席　従業員数/35人

①

②

(Photo captions)
1 / The facade in a cattle pen style; having a signboard accented with a cowboy hat.
2 / The dining area; pursuing the West in the days of pioneers as its design theme. A wagon is suspended from the ceiling.

1/家畜小屋風のファサード　カウボーイハットを配したサインボードがある
2/ダイニングエリア　開拓時代の西部がデザインのテーマ　天井からワゴンが吊り下げられている

SBARRO ⟨New York⟩

A restaurant standing on the 33rd Street, "SBARRO" serves appetizers, pasta, warm meat entrée, salad bar, Italian pastry, etc. Since it is intended for old inhabitants in the neighboring community, it has a composed atmosphere although its interior is modern. The theme colors are green, white and red — Italian national flag colors. The pizza cooking table is installed on the front side, while the cafeteria styled counter and salad bar occupy the front half of the interior space. Pieces of cheese and dressed meat are hung, while the cafeteria uses neon light.
● SBARRO (New York)
Address/581 2nd Avenue New York, N.Y.
Opened/February 1980;   Number of seats/63;   Number of employees/15

ピザを中心に アペタイザー パスタ料理 温かいミートのアントレ サラダバーやイタリアンペストリーなどのメニューで構成されるこのレストランは 33丁目(33rd Street)に位置し周辺の古くからの住人を対象としているのでモダンな中にも落ち着いた雰囲気を醸し出している。グリーン 白 赤のイタリアの国旗の色がテーマになっている。ピザの調理場を前面にして カフェテリア形式のカウンターとサラダバーが店内の前半分を占めている。チーズや加工肉をぶらさげたり カフェテリア部分にはネオンが用いられている。
●スバーロ ⟨ニューヨーク⟩
Address/581 2nd Avenue New York, N.Y. 開店/1980年2月 客席数/63席 従業員数/15人

(Photo captions)
1 / The cafeteria and dining area viewed from the salad bar in the center; the interior is accented with Italian national flag colors.
2 / The dining area is modern but has a composed atmosphere.
3 / The buffet counter from whose ceiling ham, sausage, etc. are hung.

1/サラダバーを中心にカフェテリアとダイニングエリアをみる イタリアの国旗の色をテーマにまとめられている
2/モダンな中にも落ち着いた雰囲気のあるダイニング
3/ハムやソーセージがぶら下げられたビュッフェカウンター

PICNIC FOOD COURT ⟨Denver, CO.⟩

"Tabor Center" downtown Denver is a huge facility composed of "The Shops" where 63 specialty shops gather, a 32-storied office tower and "Westin Hotel." "Picnic Food Court" is situated on the highest floor of "The Shops" where about 20 international restaurants (e.g. Chinese, Japanese, French, Italian, Mexican, Mediterranean, and Scandinavian) are operating, side by side with conventional popular fast food shops. These cafeteria style restaurants whose guests use a common dining area. Table seating corners having a casual atmosphere, which can be utilized by 400 to 500 guests, are surrounded with order counters of respective restaurants/shops.

● PICNIC FOOD COURT (Denver, CO.)
Address/1201 16th Street Denver, CO. 80202

(Photo captions)
1 / The sign of the restaurant which is on the highest floor of "The Shops."
2 / The dining area having a casual atmosphere; table seating corners which can be used by 400 to 500 guests are surrounded with order counters of restaurants/shops.

デンバーのダウンタウンの「Tabor Center」は63店の専門店とレストランが集まる「The Shops」と 32階建のオフィスタワー そして「Westin Hotel」で構成されている施設である。「ピクニック フード コート」は「The Shops」の最上階に位置し 従来のポピュラーなアイテムを売るファーストフード店と中国 日本 フランス イタリア メキシコ料理に加え 地中海や北欧料理などインターナショナルな料理店が20店ほど出店しており 共通のダイニングエリアを使用する カフェテリア形式のレストランである。400～500人が利用できるカジュアルな雰囲気のテーブル席のまわりを 各店のオーダーカウンターが取り囲んでいる。

●ピクニック フード コート〈コロラド・デンバー〉
Address/1201 16th Street Denver, CO.80202

1/「The Shops」の最上階にあるレストランのサイン
2/カジュアルな雰囲気のダイニングエリア 400～500人が利用できるテーブル席のまわりにを各店のオーダーカウンターが取り囲んでいる

THE MARKET ⟨New York⟩

The 59-storied "Citycorp Center" in the center of Manhattan has a shopping/restaurant facility called "The Market" across three floors. It is composed of 20 shops, including restaurants, a bookstore, a furniture shop, a tableware shop, a tobacco shop and a flower shop. Onto the center courtyard the banded sunlight streams in through a sky light, reflecting on the trees, glass wall, etc. As the sun moves, shadows and brightness vary. At the white tables with white chairs, guests enjoy drinks and foods ordered from the adjacent restaurants or snack bars. From evening till night the courtyard is filled with people who gather to enjoy events performed on the stage. Thus, the courtyard serves as an "international bazar" in midtown New York.

● THE MARKET (New York)
Address/One Citycorp Center, New York, N.Y. 10043

マンハッタンの中央部の地上59階建の「シティコープ センター」の中に3層に渡って「The Market」と呼ばれるショッピングとレストランの施設がある。レストラン 書店 家具店 食器店 煙草店 花店などの20店で構成されている。中央に設けられた中庭には 天窓から帯状の太陽光がさしこみ 樹々やガラスの壁に反射し 太陽の動きとともに影や明るさに変化ができる。白い椅子とテーブルには まわりのレストランやスナックから持ち出したテイクアウトオーダーの飲物や食事を楽しむ風景が見られ 夕方から夜にかけては ステージで催されるイベントを楽しむ人たちでいっぱいになる。ニューヨークのミッドタウンにおける"インターナショナル バザール"と呼ばれるスポットになっている。

● ザ マーケット ⟨ニューヨーク⟩
Address/One Citycorp Center, New York, N.Y. 10043

(Photo captions)
1 / The courtyard installed under light which comes in through a sky light on the stairwell through 7 floors.
2・3 / The restaurant and shopping facilities around the atrium terrace.
4 / The atrium terrace; since it is opened to the general public, it is crowded with people who come to enjoy eating and drinking, or take rest. In the evening, a music concert or show is held.

1/7階の吹き抜けの天窓からさしこむ光の下に設けられた中庭
2・3/アトリウムのテラスを囲んでレストランとショッピングの施設がある
4/アトリウムのテラス 一般に開放され 食事や飲物を楽しんだり 憩いの場として集う人たちでいっぱいになる。夕方になると音楽会やショーが催される

INTERNATIONAL FOOD WORKS ⟨Atlanta, Georgia⟩

A huge (having about 18,000 sq. ft. or 5,500 m² of space and capable of accommodating 500 guests) self-service restaurant. In the center of the restaurant, eight pavilions having different names and concept menus are installed. While introducing trees, the interior is accepted with colors such as red, yellow and green, and designed to look like a bright, spacious green house. The ceiling whose height corresponds to 2 floors, is finished with objets which look like floating Western kites.
- INTERNATIONAL FOOD WORKS
  (Atlanta, Georgia)
Address/Georgia Pacific Center, 133 Perchtree Street Atlanta, Georgia 30303
Opened/August 1982;   Number of seats/500;   Number of employees/50

アトランタのダウンタウンの50階建の「ジョージア パシフィックセンタービル」の2階にある500席 18,000平方フィート（約5,500m²）という広大なスペースを持つセルフサービスレストランである。レストランの中央部に 8つのそれぞれ異なる名前とコンセプトメニューを持つパビリオンを設けている。樹木を持ち込み 赤 黄 緑などのカラーをアクセントに 明るい広がりのあるグリーンハウスといった店内構成になっている。2層分の高さを持たせた天井の空間にはカラフルな西洋凧が遊泳しているような演出をしている。
● インターナショナル フード ワークス〈ジョージア・アトランタ〉
Address/Georgia Pacific Center, 133 Peachtree Street Atlanta, Georgia 30303　開店/1982年8月　客席数/500席　従業員数/50人

(Photo caption)
The bright dining area designed to introduce natural light from the high ceiling; colorful kites are floating under the ceiling.

自然光の入る高い空間を持つダイニングエリア 天井にはカラフルな西洋凧が舞う

FULTON MARKET 〈New York〉

"FULTON MARKET" stands facing East River Quay which is close to Wall Street on the southernmost end of Manhattan Island. Here, there was a port which prospered with international trade by the mid-19th century, but has been redeveloped according to the "South Street Seaport" project which is intended to preserve old culture. 13 specialty food shops are open on the 1st floor of a 3-storied building, while restaurants and bars are on the 1st floor, mezzanine and 3rd floor. All of the 2nd floor is called "Finger Foods & Specialty" which is composed of 22 variety restaurants and spacious table seating corners specializing in ethnic foods and their takeout service. Since the opening, "FULTON MARKET" has drawn hot attention of New Yorkers and tourists.
● FULTON MARKET (New York)
Address/South Street New York, N.Y.
Opened/July 1983

マンハッタン島の最南端のウォール街に近いイーストリバーの埠頭に面して「フルトン マーケット」はある。19世紀半ばまで栄えた貿易港があった場所で 古い文化を残すための"サウス ストリート シーポート"計画により再開発されたもの。3階建の建物の1階には 13の食品専門店が出店している。レストランとバーは1階 中2階 3階にある。2階の全フロアは"フィンガー フーズ＆スペシャリティ"と呼ばれ エスニック料理とアメリカン料理のテイクアウトを専門にした22店のバラエティ レストラン群と広いテーブル席のコーナーで構成されており オープン以来 ニューヨーカーや観光客の人気を集めている。
●フルトン マーケット〈ニューヨーク〉
Address/South Street Seaport New York, N.Y.
開店/1983年7月

(Photo captions)
1/ The facade of "FULTON MARKET"; reproduced the architecture and design in the 18th century.
2〜5/ The central stairwell is accented with fish decor under which open ethnic food restaurants are installed.

1/18世紀当時の建築とデザインを再現した「フルトン マーケット」のファサード
2〜5/中央吹き抜けの部分に魚のデコアが飾られ その下にオープンなエスニック料理店が並ぶ

Index

■ **NEW YORK**

ALO ALO : 1030 3rd Avenue, 61st Street & 3rd Avenue New York, N.Y. 10021
☎212-838-4343 ··64
BAYAMO : 707 Broadway North of 4th Street New York, N.Y. ☎212-475-5151 ··············12
＊BENIHANA CAFE ···52
BICE : 7 East 54th Street New York, N.Y. 1002 ☎212-688-1999·······················84
＊THE CAFE AT BETWEEN THE BREAD ···220
CAFE IGUANA : 235 Park Avenue South at 19th Street New York, N.Y. 10003
☎212-529-4770 ···14
CHINA GRILL : 60 West 53rd Street, between 5th & 6th Avenue, New York,
N.Y. 10019 ☎212-333-7788 ··20
＊EL INTERNACIONAL ···24
EL TEDDY'S : 219 West Broadway New York, N.Y. 10013 ☎212-941-7070 ···············22
FULTON MARKET : South Street Seaport New York, N.Y. ······································236
LE MADRI : 168 West 18th Street New York, N.Y. 10011 ☎212-727-8022··············82
MALVASIA : 185 East 60th Street New York, N.Y. 10022 ☎212-233-4790 ················72
THE MARKET : One Citycorp Center, New York, N.Y. 10043·······························232
MESA GRILL : 102 Fifth Avenue New York, N.Y. 10011 ☎212-807-7400 ···············134
Restaurant & Bar at MORGANS : 237 Madison Avenue New York ,N.Y. 10016a
☎212-686-0300 ···153
＊MÖVENPIC···188
＊MUSTANG GRILL ···168
101 THINGS TO EAT : 101 Park Avenue New York ,N.Y. 10178 ····························221
PALIO : 151 West 51st Street New York, N.Y. 10019 ☎212-245-4850·····················68
PIPELINE : 225 Liberty Street, 2 World Financial Center, New York, N.Y. 10281
☎212-945-2755 ···140
REMI : 145 West 53rd Street New York, N.Y. 10019 ☎212-581-4242 ···················66
＊ROBBIN'S ··148
SATURNIA : 54 Varick Street New York, N.Y. 10013 ☎212-966-1239·················154
SBARRO : 581 2nd Avenue New York, N.Y. ··229
SFUZZI : 53 West 65th Street New York, N.Y. 10023 ☎212-873-3700 ···················76
TOMMY TANG'S : 323 Greenwich Street New York, N.Y. 10013 ☎212-334-9190 ···········32
TRATTORIA DELL'ARTE : 900 7th Avenue at 57th Street New York, N.Y.
☎212-245-9800 ···70
THE 21 CLUB : 21 West 52nd Street New York, N.Y.···110
WINDOWS ON THE WORLD : 107th floor New York Manhattan One World Trade
Center bldg, New York, N.Y.···184

■ **LOS ANGELES**

AKASAKA HANTEN : 123 S.Weller Street 2nd floor Los Angeles, CA. 90012 ···············56
CAMELIONS : 246 26th Street Santa Monica, CA. 9002 ☎213-395-0746 ···············120
CARDINI : Los Angeles Hilton Hotel, 930 Wilshire Boulevard Los Angeles, CA. 90017
☎213-629-4321(3550)···88
CHA CHA CHA : 656 N.Virgil Avenue Los Angeles, CA. 90004 ☎213-664-7223 ···········26
CHAMPAGNE : 10506 Santa Monica Boulevard Los Angeles, CA. 90025
☎213-470-8446···122
LA CHAUMIERE : Century Plaza Hotel, 2025 Avenue of The Stars City Los Angeles,
CA. 90067 ☎213-277-2000 ··100
＊CHINA CLUB···54
CHOPSTIX : 7229 Melrose Avenue Los Angeles, CA. 90046 ☎213-937-1111 ···············60
CITRUS : 6703 Melrose Avenue Los Angeles, CA. 90038 ☎213-857-0034 ················126
CITY GRILL : Los Angeles Hilton & Towers, 930 Wilshire Boulevard Los Angeles,
CA. 90017 ☎213-623-5971···166
DC 3 : 2800 Donald Douglas Loop North Santa Monica, CA. 90405 ☎213-399-2323 ···132
＊DDL FOODSHOW··74
EL MOCAMBO : 8338 W.Third Street Los Angeles, CA. 90048 ☎213-651-2113 ·············34
EL TORIDO : 9595 Wilshire Boulevard Beverly Hills, CA. 90210 ☎213-550-1559···········28
FLAKEY JAKE'S : 2347 Sepulveda West Los Angeles, CA. 90025 ☎206-644-9467 ····222
FRAGRANT VEGETABLE RESTAURANT : 11589 Wilshire Boulevard Los Angeles, CA.
☎213-312-1442 ···58

American restaurants introduced in this book are classified by location. Data such as name and telephone number of each restaurant denote those collected at the time of publication of the book, and some of them may have changed. Kindly understand any such change. The book has also included restaurants which, although closed now, have characteristic designs and concepts. These restaurants are differentiated by ＊ mark.

May 1992

Graphic-sha editorial staff

HAMLET GARDENS : 1139 Glendon of Lindbook Westwood Los Angeles,
　　　　　　CA. 90024 ☎213-824-1818 ･･････････････････････････････････214
HARD ROCK CAFE : 8600 Beverly Boulevard Los Angeles, CA. ･･････････････152
＊KANSAI SUSHI KAPPO ･･･50
KISHO-AN : Beverly Center Top floor 131 N.La Chienega Boulevard Los Angeles,
　　　　　　CA. 90044 ･･･48
KYOTARU : 8649 Firestone Boulevard Downey, CA. 90241 ･･････････････････46
LANGAN'S BRASSERIE : 10250 Santa Monica Boulevard Los Angeles, CA.90067
　　　　　　☎213-785-0961 ･･･194
MA MAISON : 8555 Beverly Boulevard Los Angeles, CA. 90048 ☎213-655-1991 ･･･････112
THE OLD SPAGHETTI FACTORY : 5939 Sunset Boulevard Holywood, CA. ････････92
L'ORANGERIE : 903 North La Chinega Boulevard Los Angles, CA. ･･････････114
＊PINAFINI ･･･80
REBECCA'S : 2025 Pacific Avenue Venice, CA. 90028 ☎213-306-6266 ････････16
THE RED ONION : 4215 Admiralty Way Marina Del Ray, CA. 90291 ･････････42
RED ROBIN : 4232 Katella Avenue Los Angeles, CA. 90270 ☎213-594-4601 ･････210
＊THE RITZ CAFE ･･･180
SALADS PLUS : 577 North Mountain Upland, CA. ･･････････････････････････218
SPAGO CALIFORNIA CUISINE : 8795 Sunset BouleVard Los Angeles, CA. 90069 ･･･････146
ST.JAMES'S CLUB : 8358 Sunset Boulevard Los Angeles, CA. 90069
　　　　　　☎213-654-7100 ･･･164
＊TUMBLEWEED ･･･150
VICTORIA STATION : 100 Universal City Plaza Universal City, CA. ･･････････206

■ SAN FRANCISCO
ACAPULCO Y LOS ARCOS : Larkspur, CA. ････････････････････････････････40
THE AVENUE GRILL : 44 E.Bithedale Mill Valley, CA. 94941 ☎415-388-6003 ･････176
BRAVO FONO : Stanford Shopping Center,99 Palatine Court Palo Alto, CA. ･･････190
CAMPTON PLACE : 340 Stockton Street San Francisco, CA. 94108 ☎415-781-5555 ････182
CORINTIA : Ramada Renaissance Hotel,55 City Magnin Street San Francisco,
　　　　　　CA. 94102・2865 ☎415-392-8000 ･････････････････････････90
FOURNOU'S OVEN : Nob Hill San Francisco, CA. 94108 ･･････････････････118
＊JIL'S RESTAURANT ･･･104
IL FORNAIO 'GASTRONOMIA ITALIANA' : Levis Plaza, 1265 Battery Street
　　　　　　San Francisco, CA.94111 ☎415-986-0100 ･･････86
LASCAUX : 248 Sutter Street San Francisco, CA. ☎415-391-1555 ･･･････････102
＊MAXWELL'S PLUM ･･･98
POSTRIO RESTAURANT : 545 Post Street San Francisco, CA. 94102
　　　　　　☎415-776-7825 ･･･158
ROSALIE'S : 1415 Van Ness Avenue San Francisco, CA.94109 ☎415-928-7188 ･･････130
ROTUNDA RESTAURANT : 150 Stockton San Francisco, CA. ･･････････････････96
RUSTY SCUPPER : 1800 Montgomery San Francisco, CA. ･･･････････････････198
690 SPEEDO : 690 Van Ness Avenue San Francisco, CA. 94102 ☎415-255-6900 ･･････138

■ CALIFORNIA
BISTANGO : 19100 Von Karman Avenue Irvine, CA. 92715 ☎714-752-5222 ･･････142
COOK BOOK : EL TORO,CA. ･･200
DON JOSE : 21227 Hawthorne Boulevard,Torrance, CA. 90503 ･･････････････36
555 EAST : 555 East Ocean Boulevard Long Beach, CA. 90802 ☎213-497-0626 ･･････170
＊FORTY CARROTS ･･･202
THE O-GAME PIZZA CORRAL : 9365 Monte Vista Avenue Montclair, CA. 91763 ･･････228
RAINBOW PIER FISH MARKET : 423 Shoreline Village Drive Long Beach,
　　　　　　CA. 90802 ･･204
THE RED ONION : 16450 Pacific Coast Highway Huntington Beach, CA. 92649 ･･････38
SALUD : 11707 Beach Boulevard Huntington Beach, CA. 924647 ☎714-842-1194 ･････30
THE SKYROOM : The Breakers Hotel,210 East Ocean Boulevard Long Beach,
　　　　　　CA. 90802 ☎213-432-8781 ･･････････････････････････････106
THE VELVET TURTLE : 17555 Casleton City of Industry, CA. 91745 ･････････196
WELDON'S : 250 S.Bistol Street Costa Mesa, CA. 92626 ･････････････････224

本書に掲載されたアメリカのレストラン
を所在地別に分類しています。
店名 電話番号などは 本書発行時のも
ので 現在変更されている場合もありま
すので ご了承下さい。 なお現在閉店さ
れているレストランでも 特徴のあるデ
ザインやコンセプトの店は収録してあり
ますが その場合は店名のはじめに＊印
をつけ区別しました。
　　　　　　　　　　　1992年5月
　　　　　　　　グラフィック社 編集部

■CHICAGO
* ＊AMÉRIQUE ……………………………………………………………………………136
* BISTRO 110：110 East Peason Street Chicago, Illinois 60611 ☎312-266-3110 ……178
* THE BUTCHER SHOP：West Ontario Chicago,Illinois 60611 ☎312-440-4900 ……174
* CAFE BA・BA・REEBA!：2024 N.Holated Chicago, Illinois 60614 ☎312-935-5000 ……44
* ＊CAFE 21 ……………………………………………………………………………124
* D.B.KAPLAN'S：Water Tower Place 7th floor,845 North Michigan Avenue
  Chicago, Illinois 60611 ……………………………………………………208
* DON ROTH'S RIVER PLAZA：405 N.Wabash Chicago, Illinois ………………………186
* GORDON：500 North Clark Street Chicago, Illinois 60610 ☎312-467-9780 ……162
* JIM MACMAHON'S：1970 North Lincoln Avenue Chicago, Illinois 60614
  ☎312-751-1700 ………………………………………………………………156
* McDONALD'S：600 North Clark Street Chicago, Illinois 60610 ☎312-664-7940 ……226
* OUT TAKES：16 West Ontario Chicago, Illinois 60610 ☎312-951-7979 ……………160
* SCOOZI：410 West Huron Street Chicago, Illinois 60610 ☎312-943-5900 ……78
* ＊STELLA'S PLACE ……………………………………………………………………144

■ATLANTA
* INTERNATIONAL FOOD WORKS：Georgia Pacific Center,133 Peachetree Street
  Atlanta, Georgia ……………………………………234
* THE PINK PEAR：369 Sandy Spring Circle Atlanta, Georgia 30328 ☎404-256-5589 ……193

■DALLAS
* ZUCCHINI'S: The Westin Hotel Galleria Dallas, Parkway at LBJ Freeway, Texas ……192

■DENVER
* ORGAN GRINDER：2370 W.Alemeda Boulevard Denver, Colorado 80223 ……212
* PICNIC FOOD COURT：1201 16th Street Denver, Colorado 80202 ……………230

■NEW ORLEANS
* HENRI：Hotel Meridien New Orleans, 614 Canal Street New Orleans, Louisiana 70130
  ☎504-527-7808 ……………………………………………………………………108

■ORLANDO
* CASA GALLARDO：8250 International Drive Orlando, Florida 32809 ………………18

■WASHINGTON D.C.
* THE COLONNADE RESTAURANT：2401 M.Street N.W.Washington D.C. 20037
  ☎202-429-2400 …………………………………………………………116

レストラン デザイン-1
セレクテッド アメリカン レストラン

1992年5月25日　初版第1刷発行

定価	12,500円（本体 12,136円）
著者	斎藤　武
発行者	久世利郎
印刷・製本	凸版印刷株式会社
写植	有限会社福島写植
英文	株式会社海広社
協力	
レイアウト	はとおく社
カバーデザイン	ウイークエンド株式会社
発行所	株式会社グラフィック社
	〒102 東京都千代田区九段北1-9-12
	電話03-3263-4318 振替・東京3-114345

本書を無断で複写(コピー)することは 著作権法上認められている場合を除き 禁じられています。
落丁・乱丁はお取り替え致します。

ISBN4-7661-0684-9 C2092 P12500E